PR

"... the first in what has the potential to be a fascinating trilogy of general appeal. McGee's simple narrative belies the novel's complexity, a factor that will make this intriguing book accessible to a wide variety of teen readers."

—*Booklist*

"McGee's versatility as an author really shines with this latest offering ... *Anomaly* ... should encourage inspirational romance readers who haven't yet tried out dystopian lit to give it a shot."

—USAToday.com

"*Anomaly* grabs the reader and refuses to let go. From the introduction to misunderstood anomaly, Thalli, to the boy she loves, one is never completely sure what is fact and what is a horrifying virtual reality. This is sure to be a favorite of teens everywhere."

—Heather Burch, author of the critically acclaimed Halflings series

"A razor-edged look at the resilience of Christian faith, *Anomaly* is taut, high-stakes dystopia that grips on the first page and twists all the way through."

—Evan Angler, author of the Swipe series

"*Anomaly* is a fabulous read! Krista McGee is a fresh and gifted voice in YA apocalyptic fiction. Excellent characters and an intriguing plot provide readers with great entertainment—as well as a call to go 'outside' themselves. I can't wait for book two!"

—Kathryn Mackel, author of *Boost*

"A beautiful story that has me wondering if I would have the strength to be an Anomaly. Fans of James Dashner's *Maze Runner* will love Krista McGee's *Anomaly*."

—Jon Lewis, author of the C.H.A.O.S. trilogy

ACCLAIM FOR KRISTA MCGEE

"McGee's debut novel is an absolute gem. Anyone who enjoys reality television and a well-told story shouldn't hesitate to read this great book."

—*Romantic Times* TOP PICK! Review of *First Date*

"[A] touching, fun, edifying, campy, quick and downright delicious teen read."

—USAToday.com regarding *First Date*

"Good things come to those who wait—and pray."

—*Kirkus Reviews* regarding *Starring Me*

"An abundance of real-life problems . . . should keep this story relevant for many teens."

—*Publisher's Weekly* review of *Right Where I Belong*

LUMINARY

OTHER NOVELS BY KRISTA MCGEE

Anomaly

First Date
Starring Me
Right Where I Belong

LUMINARY

BOOK TWO IN THE ANOMALY TRILOGY

KRISTA MCGEE

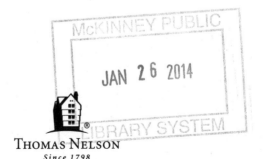

THOMAS NELSON
Since 1798

NASHVILLE   DALLAS   MEXICO CITY   RIO DE JANEIRO

Published in Nashville, Tennessee, by Thomas Nelson. Thomas Nelson is a registered trademark of Thomas Nelson, Inc.

Thomas Nelson, Inc., titles may be purchased in bulk for educational, business, fund-raising, or sales promotional use. For information, please e-mail SpecialMarkets@ThomasNelson.com.

Publisher's Note: This novel is a work of fiction. Names, characters, places, and incidents are either products of the author's imagination or used fictitiously. All characters are fictional, and any similarity to people living or dead is purely coincidental.

Scripture quotations are from THE NEW KING JAMES VERSION. © 1982 by Thomas Nelson, Inc. Used by permission. All rights reserved.

Library of Congress Cataloging-in-Publication Data

McGee, Krista, 1975-
 Luminary / by Krista McGee.
  pages cm. — (Anomaly trilogy ; book 2)
 Summary: Able to experience emotions that should have been eradicated by genetic modification, Thalli must journey across an unknown land to find a hidden civilization of people actually born to families.
 ISBN 978-1-4016-8874-5 (pbk.)
 [1. Emotions—Fiction. 2. Families--Fiction. 3. Love—Fiction. 4. Christian life—Fiction. 5. Science fiction.] I. Title.
 PZ7.M4784628Lu 2014
 [Fic]—dc23   2013029517

Printed in the United States of America

14 15 16 17 18 RRD 5 4 3 2 1

To my mother, Pamela Brush Henderson.
Thank you for always encouraging me to develop
my talents and my imagination.
I love you!

PROLOGUE

Our four travelers haven't stopped moving yet." Dr. Loudin continues to stare at the screen, his gaze following the four green dots that represent Thalli, Berk, Rhen, and John. "That's a good sign."

"Yes, but it's only been a few days." Dr. Williams picks up an orange and slowly peels it. The other Scientists continue eating, their gazes darting from the screen back to their plates.

"We have a problem." Dr. Grenz enters the Scientists' eating quarters, and every pair of eyes rests on him. "James is dying."

The room is silent. One Scientist already died suddenly. Medical tests were run on each of the remaining Nine after his death. All were healthy. With continued genetic treatment and medications, the Scientists anticipate their life spans will be well over one hundred years.

"Impossible." Dr. Williams places both hands flat on the table as she stands. "He was just here—two days ago, when we watched the four leave the State. He was fine then. He probably just has a slight sickness."

"He's been working in the medical center in Pod C since then, studying data and compiling research. He collapsed an hour ago. He was barely able to call me on his communications pad." Dr. Grenz sighs. "His symptoms are exactly the same as the others who have died from oxygen deprivation. We simply cannot sustain life down here anymore."

"Which is why we allowed our four travelers to escape aboveground." Dr. Loudin points to the screen where the green dots continue to move south. "They have everything they need to find our rogue Scientists. Once they find them, we bring them here. Together, we will find a solution to the oxygen problem."

"So all our lives depend on them?" Dr. Grenz shakes his head. "What about James? No one knows more about genetics than he does. We lose him, we lose all his knowledge. How do we replace that?"

"We don't lose James." Dr. Loudin's face is red, his eyes bloodshot as he tears them away from the screen to look at Dr. Grenz. "If he needs new lungs, then give him new lungs. Take them from someone in Pod A. Replace the heart as well. There is no reason we cannot ensure his survival."

"But the oxygen levels—" Dr. Grenz groans. "Why don't we just leave with them? Return aboveground?"

"No!" Dr. Loudin stands, his voice echoing in the large

room. "Have you forgotten why we created the State? The world we grew up in was destroying itself, day after day in a billion different ways. We created a new world with order and peace. If we return above now, then we forfeit all of this. The world—those pockets of survivors—will take us back to where we were forty years ago. Is that what you want?"

"Of course not."

"Exactly." Dr. Loudin takes a deep breath. "So we find the Scientists who left us, bring them back, and work together to repair the State. We find out what those pockets of survivors have and what they need. Then we give them what they need. We become as indispensable above as we are below. Then we can infiltrate every corner of the world. Then—and only then—we can ensure that the world will move forward according to our vision."

Dr. Williams nods. "You are right, of course. In our fear, we have forgotten our purpose."

Dr. Loudin's voice softens. "And have the Engineers work to build transports that can go farther, faster. Similar to the jet airplanes of old."

"I will give them your instructions."

"I will keep watching our four," Dr. Loudin says. "They are the key to everything."

"But what if they fail to find the Scientists?" Dr. Grenz laces his fingers together.

"They will still be useful." Dr. Loudin shrugs. "Whether they find our colleagues or not, they are still living projects—once we retrieve them, dead or alive, we can examine their bodies to determine how their organs processed life aboveground. Hopefully, they will make it past the area that is still toxic with radioactive particles so they can breathe in the atmosphere, eat food grown on the earth. Seeing how their bodies cope with the change from State-living to earth-living will better prepare us to make that transition, when and if we choose to live above."

Dr. Loudin looks around the room. "How much time do you hypothesize we have, Grenz, before our oxygen supply reaches fatal levels?"

"No more than three months." Dr. Grenz rubs his temples with his fingertips. "If we divert all the oxygen supplies to this building. We move the survivors from Pods A and B here."

"All right." Dr. Loudin nods. "Then we do that. For two months."

"*Two* months?" Dr. Grenz asks.

"Then we retrieve our travelers and, hopefully, the Scientists they will find." Loudin's eyes are once again transfixed on the screen. "We correct the problems belowground, then we move on to correct the problems aboveground. Once and for all."

CHAPTER ONE

W e need to move as quickly as possible." Berk's amplified voice fills my helmet, which protects me from the toxic air. "The Scientists will know we have left. They will send Monitors to follow us."

I can still hardly believe we are here. Outside of the State. "On transports just like this?" I imagine the torture we will all receive when we are caught. I am sure the Scientists will not allow us the painless annihilation I faced. "We should never have come."

"Thalli. It is not logical to begin this journey with a defeated attitude."

"Rhen is right." Berk's face appears in the rectangular slit at the front of my helmet.

I try not to focus on his full lips, the stubble growing along his square jaw. It is not hard—our faces are both covered with these heavy helmets, making me feel even more distant from him. His hands are on my shoulders, but, of course, I can't feel them either. Layers of protective fabric keep me from feeling anything. I think it has wrapped itself around my heart too. And my mind.

The thrill of seeing Berk? Gone. It is replaced by the crippling fear that instead of facing my own death, I will be the cause of death for these people I love.

Berk's bright green eyes force my attention back to him. "I need you to focus."

I want to slap his hands down. How dare he speak to me like that? Like he is a Scientist and I am his project? Like we are not from the same pod, the same generation? Like he has not lived the same seventeen years I have? If nothing else good comes from it, being aboveground means that he has no authority. We are escaping the rule of the Scientists.

Berk sighs and turns away. The weight of his hands on my shoulders is gone, replaced by a heavier weight in my heart. What is wrong with me? Why am I behaving like this?

I do not have time to examine my feelings because John appears. His bushy white eyebrows are so close to the glass of his helmet they appear magnified, making his crystal-blue eyes seem smaller in comparison, the wrinkles surrounding his eyes even more visible. If I had the energy, I might laugh. But I don't have the energy. Or the desire.

"Just leave me here." I step away from John. "Go back down,

tell them you were forced. Tell them it was my idea that you rescued me, then return to the State on your own. We don't all need to die."

John places a gloved hand on top of my helmet. "No one is leaving you, Thalli."

I want to argue, but I feel my arm being pulled, hands around my waist lifting me up. I turn and see Berk placing me on a transport.

"I said I want you to leave me."

Berk stands in front of me, his eyes hard. "You are coming on this transport with the rest of us."

He pushes me toward the corner of the transport. He is taking me prisoner. Just like a Scientist. He was designed to take charge and have all the answers. But that was below. Anger burns inside me. I move to step off, but Rhen and John block me.

"We need four people to steer this." Rhen is still calm, irritatingly calm, but she is firm. She may be slight in stature, but she is strong in other ways. Even John refuses to move.

I do not think she is right. We do not need four people to steer the transport. I think they are trying to force me on by making me believe I am necessary. If I thought my refusing would cause them to leave me behind, I would refuse. But I know they will not leave me behind. And the longer we wait to leave, the sooner the Monitors will find us. I step back into place. They should never have brought me here. The Scientists will find us. They will kill each one of them before me, just to punish me for bringing them here. I slam my hand into the column beside me and the transport tips precariously to the side.

"We have to work together or we'll never get off the

ground." Berk's voice has softened, but he is still behaving like a Scientist, still giving orders and expecting me to obey them.

"Look up, Thalli. Look at what the Designer has done. Trust him."

I do as John says, tipping my helmet far back. The sky is a deep blue, and there are darker clouds hovering throughout. I turn my head and see the moon. Not the simulation of the moon I saw in Progress, but the actual moon, the way I have always wanted to see it. It is huge and white, not smooth like I imagined it. Imperfect.

"We need to go." Berk interrupts my thoughts.

"Give her a moment, son. The Creator of all this is in control, Thalli. We do not need to fear the Scientists. They are not more powerful than the Designer."

I want so much to believe John, but fear keeps my stomach in knots and my shallow breath overrides that desire. My head aches, and I want to lie down on the transport and sleep. Forever. But I cannot lie down. I cannot sleep. I have to keep moving.

Slowly, the transport lifts off the ground. I do as Berk says, leaning in and out against the column, because if I refuse to go, the others will be caught with me. Our only hope is to outrun the Monitors. I try to pray that we can do just that, but I have no words, just emotions that overwhelm me, clouding every thought.

I try to think about something else. The transport shifts beneath me, and I recall the only other time I was on one of these: When I woke up and had no feeling in my arm. Back when Berk was kind to me, when he didn't treat me like he was the Scientist and I was the subordinate. When we spent our days together. When I felt so much love for him I thought my heart would burst. I had to lie on a transport like this one, wrapped in a medical blanket, so I could be examined by the Scientists.

"How do you know where to go?" I try to remain calm. But we are aboveground, where no one has been for over forty years.

A greenish grid comes to life in front of my eyes. It is so close, it takes a few seconds for my eyes to adjust. It is a map of some sort.

"See the orange dots?" Berk asks. They are tiny, like needle pricks. But I see them. "Those are communities who survived the War."

"No one survived the War." I repeat what I have been taught since infancy. The earth was destroyed by the Nuclear War over four decades ago. The whole earth. Only The Ten—Scientists who had been building an underground State—survived. The only people left on earth were those of us created in the Scientists' laboratories. The Scientists prepared for the possibility of a nuclear war and everything, including the ingredients for the creation of children, had been stored underground, protected. Berk, Rhen, and I were all created below. Only John was from the time before, when children were "born" in the primitive way.

"Thalli, you know the Scientists aren't always truthful." Berk's sharp reply brings with it terrible memories. The Scientists tricked me into believing there was a colony right here, above the State. I had seen the people there, touched them, experienced this colony, only to find out it was a cerebral manipulation. It wasn't real.

"I found this map hidden among the Scientists' data. They didn't want anyone to know about it."

"But you knew, of course." I hear myself saying this to Berk, hear the caustic tone. I hate it, but I cannot stop it.

Berk releases a short breath. "I have been finding many things in the last few weeks. Some of those helped save your life."

"Save it for what?" I shout into my helmet. "So we can spend a few hours on the toxic earth before we're discovered and killed back in the State?"

"You are allowing fear to control you." John's voice is quiet but filled with authority. "This is not the Thalli I know."

I choose not to speak. He is right. I am not the same. I am not sure I will ever be the same again. I look down—at a gray, ashen ground receding below us. It looks the same in every direction. Flat, dry, gray. Even the sky is gray, the clouds filling in whatever blue spaces had been there.

"What do you suppose the Scientists want to do with this map?" Rhen asks.

"They are monitoring the pockets of survivors."

"So they can relocate?"

"They are not interested in relocating anytime soon," Berk replies, as the transport levels out. "They can't control people up here. There's too much space. Too much freedom. I think they prefer the confines of the State. That's why they were so excited about yours and Thalli's music simulation. They are hopeful they can use that data to find a solution to the oxygen crisis."

I remember that simulation. Rhen was trapped. In my music. It was awful. But she broke free. How the Scientists can use that, I do not know. I do know that music is powerful. Music pointed me to the Designer, spoke to me in ways logic never could. That music could also solve the Scientists' dilemma seems very plausible.

"How soon do you think the Monitors will catch up with us?" I look behind us, expecting to see another transport, weapons drawn to attack.

"Don't think about that." Berk pushes the transport harder. I grab the column to keep from slipping to the center. "We are traveling as fast as we can, and we started before them. My hope is they'll give up, assume we'll die out here."

I scan the horizon again. Gray. Barren. "A good assumption."

"Their intention was to kill us anyway." Rhen sounds like she is solving a calculus equation, not discussing our chances of survival. "I imagine they would prefer not to waste resources searching for us when there is so much need below."

"We are defying them." I want to shake Rhen. "And we're escaping the State. No one has ever been allowed to do either of those things."

"We can't worry about what *might* happen," John says. "Let's just press forward. We will deal with the Monitors if they come."

"So where are we going?" Rhen asks.

The grid moves south, then east. "See that pocket there? It is the closest to us. About nine hundred miles away."

"Nine hundred miles?" I don't even know how to calculate that distance. It seems astronomical. The entire State is not more than ten miles from one end to the other.

"This transport can move at about twenty-five miles an hour."

"That's thirty-six hours." Rhen figures it out before I can begin putting the numbers into an equation in my brain.

"We can't drive the whole time." There is no room on this transport for any of us to sleep, even if we wanted to. "It could take a whole week to get there."

"I brought enough food for two weeks." Berk's calm voice just makes me angry.

"And then what?" My breath is fogging the eyepiece in my helmet. "What if we get there and find those orange dots were wrong?"

"Then we go to the next pocket." The grid shifts to the east. "It's only about sixty miles from the pocket we're going to."

I take a deep breath. "Why are there two pockets sixty miles from each other and none around here for nine hundred miles?"

"There are several others to the north of us, but the climate would be difficult for our bodies. It is warmer in the south. We'd do better there."

Of course Berk has thought this through. I should trust him. He is brilliant. He knows what he is doing. Why am I so angry? I shouldn't feel this way. But I don't know how *not* to feel this way. I am not the same person I was below, in the annihilation chamber. I was better then. Stronger. Up here, I am broken, useless.

"So what is the plan, Dr. Berk?"

I turn my head to look at John. I can sense the joy radiating off of him. He is relaxed. He has longed for this. For forty years. This was his home before the War. If he is disappointed to see it ravaged, he doesn't show it.

"I thought we'd try to travel eight hours each day."

I do the math this time. Two hundred miles a day. Five days, four nights. Why not travel twelve hours a day and arrive in three days and two nights? I look at John. That's why. Standing for eight hours will exhaust him. John is old. Over ninety. His body will ache from this travel. Berk has thought of that too. Of course.

"Excellent plan." Rhen understands also. Even she is kinder than I. They never should have done this, never should have risked their lives for me.

My mind drifts again to the annihilation chamber. To death. To heaven. Maybe I shouldn't, but I long for it, wish for it. John says heaven is perfect. There is no pain there, no fear. I wouldn't have to worry about my friends, wouldn't have to live in fear of being caught and returned to the State. Death seems so much easier than what faces us now. And will it come anyway? Will death by annihilation be replaced with death by upper earth?

Perhaps. Those orange dots seem so far. And so unstable. They blink and move. Are they friendly? Angry? Murderous? Of course they are primitive. And primitive people are dangerous. That's what I've always been taught. So are we leaving danger to face danger?

I tap the glass on my visor, forcing the map to disappear. I don't want to think about it anymore. Death is coming. I am more and more sure of it as we travel on. We have gotten ourselves in a hopeless situation. Berk was thinking with his heart, not his head. He was acting like me. And that is never wise.

CHAPTER TWO

T exas." John breaks the silence that hung over us for the last hour of travel.

"What?" I ask, my voice sounding like a broken violin string through the helmet.

"We are going to Texas." The green map pops up on my visor once again. The orange blinking dots seem to mock us. "Before the War this whole area was called the United States."

We all know this, of course. That information was part of our history lessons. We saw on our learning pads recordings of these Americans—always yelling at each other, angry, complaining about their living conditions, their working conditions. This was part of what the Scientists sought to eradicate. People cannot be productive with so much emotion.

"Texas." John laughs. "People there were unique. It's fitting that two colonies in Texas have survivors."

"Tell us about them," Berk says, unleashing a forty-five-minute sociology lesson from John.

If I knew how to turn off the volume in my helmet, I would. Instead, I have to listen to stories about hearty people, about a place called the Alamo, about cowboys and rodeos and boots. I don't really know these words, but they are forced on me anyway in this transport going south, headed toward this place that used to house independent, hardworking people who rode animals called bulls for fun and holed up in forts until they died.

I see my reflection in the mirrored surface of the helmet. My eyes appear more blue than green today. My hair hangs in limp, wavy brownish strands along the side of my face. I look the way I feel—pathetic.

"A friend of mine was from Texas, and he used to call it 'the promised land.'" John is still talking. "Fitting for us. We are escaping our own Egypt. Perhaps Texas is our promised land."

"Or maybe it's just as barren as this land." I can't hold it in any longer. I have to speak. "Maybe we'll get there and those orange dots will want to kill us. Or eat us. Maybe they are even worse than the Scientists ever were."

"The Israelites said the same kinds of things when they were making their way to the Promised Land. Let's not make the mistakes they made. Let us trust the Designer. He has worked many miracles throughout history. I believe we are about to experience another one."

I bite my lip. I won't argue with John. But I can't believe blindly the way he does. I wish I could. But I have too many questions, too many doubts. I have just begun to believe in a Designer, in a plan, a purpose for humanity. But my faith is weak. This is too much.

"We should stop here," Berk says, and the transport begins to lower to the ashen ground. "Rhen, will you help me prepare dinner? Thalli, you and John can set up the temporary chamber."

I do not want to stop. The Monitors who might be following us won't stop. They do not have a ninety-year-old man with them. They do have the impetus of the Scientists behind them, though, and I feel certain the Scientists want to bring us back, to make sure there is no possibility of anyone from the outside finding out about the State from anyone but them.

Berk clicks a button and I no longer hear him, though I know he is still talking. Through the lens in my helmet, I see him walking beside Rhen—close beside Rhen. She is leaning her head toward Berk, like she can hear him through her helmet.

"Shall we begin?" John's voice is in my ear, as happy as ever.

I try to focus on getting the temporary chamber assembled. I have never used one of these before. Never seen one. Why would we even have them? Our pods were perfectly good, safe. We had no need to leave them. Unless, like me, we had a medical issue. But then we'd go to a medical facility. I turn the white rectangle around. There is a small screen on the side. I touch it and it comes to life.

"Press the blue initiation panel," a computerized voice instructs me. I look all over. There is no blue panel. "Press the blue initiation panel."

"Be quiet!" I know the voice can't hear me, wouldn't care if it could, but I shout anyway. I throw the unassembled chamber to the ground. There is no blue initiation panel. We'll be sleeping on the dusty, diseased ground. Which is fine. Death will only come sooner if we spend our nights sucking in this horrible air. These helmets can only protect us so much. Surely the toxic fumes are already finding ways to seep into our bloodstreams.

"Here it is," John says.

Apparently, the panel is visible to everyone but me. I take a quick step back as the chamber comes to life. Its white walls are streaked with gray dirt as it rises from the ground, a cylinder-shaped chamber, large enough to house all four of us. John is on his knees checking the edges.

"What are you doing?"

John eases to his feet, his muscles likely sore from our day of travel. "Just checking. Back when I was a young man, we had something called tents, and we had to make sure they were stuck tight to the ground. I remember once—"

John's eyes lock onto mine and he stops his story. I don't know what nonverbal signals I am sending of my boredom, but they must be pretty awful, judging by the look on his face.

"This is in tight." John looks back at the chamber. "I don't know how they do it, but it's solid as a house."

I walk around the chamber, touch the walls. They are solid. Not the same kind of material as the pods back in the State, but they are sturdy. I try to find the entrance, but the entire structure is seamless. No door, no window. And I still don't see the blue panel.

"Very nice." Berk and Rhen are back. He surveys the chamber with a light in his eyes. He is happy. How can he sound so relaxed when we are about to spend our first night—ever—outside of the State, pursued, no doubt, by representatives sent from the State?

"There's no door." I declare the obvious because it seems I am the only one who realizes it.

"You're right." Berk doesn't seem upset by this fact. He puts a hand on top of the structure, and an entrance appears. "This is a brand-new development. I grabbed it from another Scientist in training."

"You stole it?"

"I couldn't exactly ask for it, could I? We needed a place to sleep. And a transport. And food. And these decontamination suits."

"Isn't stealing wrong?" I look at John.

"Let's think of it as plunder from the Egyptians." John tries to sound confident, but I can tell he is bothered by this too.

"Let's just go in and take a look around." Berk steps into the chamber. "Then we can eat and get some sleep."

I follow Berk. The chamber makes me feel relaxed. It looks familiar. Like my cube back in Pod C, but round. White walls, white floor, even white sleeping platforms. How this all fit in that tiny rectangle, I have no clue. But I am glad for it.

"This is perfect." Rhen sits on one of the platforms.

"How are we going to sleep with these helmets on?" Just the thought of it causes my neck to ache.

Berk touches the entrance and it closes, looking as seamless from the inside as it did from the outside. Then he removes his helmet.

"No!" I rush to Berk and try to shove the helmet back on his head. "What are you doing?"

Berk throws his helmet down and begins to remove mine. I push him away, but he is stronger than I am.

"Relax." Berk takes a huge breath.

I lose track of my thoughts as I take in his face—so handsome it makes my heart hurt. His light brown hair is messy from hours inside the helmet, but his green eyes are bright with joy. His face is unshaven—light whiskers in patches on his cheeks and his chin. "The air is safe in here. This was a prototype designed for Scientists who wanted to spend evenings aboveground to begin testing the atmosphere."

"So the Monitors won't have one of these?" The tightness in my chest lightens just a fraction, relief combating with anger that Berk did not tell us this earlier. "They only have the suits?"

"Correct." Berk pulls my helmet off my head. "It will take several months to make a new one."

I take a deep breath. The air is clean. "But it's a prototype?" I grip the edge of the sleeping platform. "It hasn't been tested?"

"No, it hasn't."

Rhen and John take their helmets off at the same time. Rhen takes a cautious breath. "You're sure it can withstand the travel? Being used and shut up again each night?"

"It is made from the best material. It can handle anything." Berk sits on a sleeping platform and runs his fingers through his hair. I look at this shelter, hoping Berk is right.

"Amazing." John leans forward. "I hate to be a bother, but I am quite hungry."

Berk jumps up from the platform. "Of course. The food should be ready now. We'll have to put the helmets back on, but it will only take a moment."

We go back outside, to a pit Rhen and Berk dug. Smoke is

pouring out of it. I am sure the smoke smells delicious. But, of course, I can smell nothing through this helmet.

"Another theft." I walk closer, seeing four meals in white containers at the bottom of the pit.

"We have to eat." Rhen shrugs and reaches for one of the containers. She hands it to me, then reaches for another. By the time she pulls the last one out, my stomach rumbles. I am hungry. I want to ask how these meals were cooked and stored. I saw so little on the transport, yet we now have a chamber and sleeping platforms and meals. But I don't ask because I hear another rumble. Not my stomach this time. But surely not someone else's. That loud?

I turn to see where the sound is coming from, and Rhen gasps in the speaker. And then I see what made her gasp.

Three huge animals, with red eyes and saliva dripping off sharp, fang-like teeth. These are animals unlike any I have ever seen on our learning pads. Huge heads, smaller bodies, matted gray fur. And the noises they're making are more than rumbles. They are angry sounds, hungry sounds. They have come here for their meal too.

They have come for us.

CHAPTER THREE

have never known so much fear. Not even seeing Monitors would have made me feel the way I am feeling now. The three animals are coming closer, red tongues hanging out, red eyes darting from Berk to Rhen to me to John. I don't know what to do. I am certain that if we move, they will move too. We are standing still but they are moving. Slowly. Very slowly.

I suddenly remember seeing a video lesson on animals called wolves. They traveled in packs, were fast, and ate animals much larger than themselves. Because they were considered unnecessary to the State, the Scientists did not breed any. These animals look eerily similar to those wolves on my learning pad. But these survived the War, adapted to the toxic

air. My heart beats faster. If the primitive wolves were dangerous, what will these mutated forms be like?

I see Berk from the corner of my eye. As soon as I realize
what he is doing, it is too late to stop him. He runs as fast as he
can away from us, causing the animals to follow him.

"Go back to the chamber." Berk's voice sounds so close,
coming through the speaker in my helmet. Yet he is running
so far away. "Go!"

Rhen pulls at my arm. "Thalli. He is right."

The first wolf pounces on Berk, dragging him to the gray
dirt. The animal's teeth dig into Berk's thigh.

"No!" I am running, willing the animals off Berk. But they
have surrounded him. I will not let him die for me. "Get off of
him. Get away."

"Thalli." Rhen's voice is strained. "I'm going for the transport. Come with me. You can't help him."

"I have to." Berk is fighting, kicking the wolves. But they
don't let up. They are trying to rip off his suit, get to his flesh.
They'll kill him. They'll kill Berk.

"*Stop!*" But of course they don't hear me. They don't have
speakers in their ears. I twist my helmet and rip it off, then toss
it on the ground as I run toward Berk, toward the wolves. "Get
away! Get off of him!"

The wolves look at me. They freeze. Their ears perk up, furry
triangles that point at me. The biggest one howls—a bone-melting
howl. My ears ring with the sound long after he finishes. In the
distance, another wolf responds. He is calling for more. Telling
them there is another meal here. Berk is yelling, but I only hear
muffled grunts and groans. I only see eyes full of fear and pain.

I turn around and see Rhen on the transport—high enough

to be out of the wolves' range, but close enough for her to reach out to try to pull me up.

"No." I push her away. "I have to get Berk."

Rhen grabs my hand. The wolves are charging me. I try to wrestle out of her grasp. Blood stains the right leg of Berk's white suit. I don't know how badly he is hurt, but I have to protect him, give him a chance to get to Rhen. He is struggling to his feet. I want to go help him, but I don't want the wolves following me, endangering him once again.

Rhen, refusing to release my hand, lowers the transport so it is right at my knees. I turn to look at her and she rams the transport into me, making me fall backward. We rise above the wolves, me lying flat on the transport.

"No!" I look down. The wolves howl at us. But it won't be long before they return to Berk, try to finish him off. I have to get off the transport.

I walk to the main steering column, push Rhen away. I need to go down. The panels lining the column don't have instructions. Just colors. I press the red button. We stop. I press the orange. We move to the right.

I close my eyes. "Designer. Help me." I reach for the last panel, almost at the bottom of the column. It is black, smaller than the others. I hope it isn't a self-destruct button. But I am out of options. The wolves are turning around, back toward Berk, tired of howling at us.

A siren pierces the air. I cover my bare ears with my hands. The wolves shrink backward. The biggest one howls—or at least I think he is howling. The siren is too loud to hear anything but its blaring, blaring, blaring, cutting through the sky with its razor sound.

The biggest wolf leaps off to the right, his legs moving so fast that a cloud of dust comes up behind him, hiding him from view. The other two follow quickly, one behind the other. I keep my hands over my ears and watch until I can't see the dust cloud anymore. Then I press the panel once again. The siren is off.

"Get to Berk," I shout to Rhen, my ears still ringing. "Now."

Rhen slams her finger into the purple panel and we are lowered, moving forward so we land right beside Berk. There is so much blood. I feel sick to my stomach, suddenly glad I haven't eaten. Berk's face is almost as white as his suit. Holes perforate his pants where the wolf's teeth were just moments ago.

I jump down and go to him.

His eyes are wide. He is in pain. I don't know what to do to help him. He is saying something, but I can't hear him with my helmet off.

My helmet is off!

That's what Berk is upset about. He is trying to get up, to find my helmet. I push on his shoulders. I can't let him move. He has lost too much blood already. We have to get him back to the chamber, stop the bleeding.

"I'm fine," I mouth slowly, right in front of him. "We need to take care of *you*."

Rhen is beside me, my helmet in her hand. Berk must have been giving her instructions. She places it back on my head, tightens it a little harder than necessary, and clicks it on. "What were you thinking?"

"You could have died," Berk says.

"Stop it. Both of you." I can't even believe they are upset with me. "Rhen, help me get Berk on the transport."

She is silent as we position ourselves—my arms under

Berk's arms, Rhen holding his legs. Berk groans as we lift him. His face looks even whiter, his eyes watery, blood continuing to stain his suit. We can't lose him. I can't lose him.

I nod at Rhen and she takes off. She knows we need to assess Berk's injuries and come up with a plan quickly. We reach the chamber and John is waiting. He opens it and helps Rhen and me carry Berk inside. He has found a medical unit, the contents laid out on the floor beside Berk's sleeping platform. I carefully remove Berk's helmet and my own as Rhen readies herself to care for Berk.

"Why?" Berk's voice is so quiet. It doesn't even sound like him.

I try not to let him see how frightened I am. I take a deep breath, will myself to speak without a tremor. "I'm fine, Berk." My exposure to the air is not nearly as frightening as the injury he sustained. How much blood can he stand to lose? What diseases might those animals carry?

"The air . . ."

"It's fine." I can say this honestly. I didn't have time to think about it while I was out there, but I realize it was not terribly different than the air in the State. Clean. Dusty, yes. But it left no aftertaste.

"We haven't run tests." Berk is barely staying conscious. "We don't know if it's fine."

I need to keep him angry, worried, to keep him awake. "So maybe I'll turn hairy and red-eyed." I shrug.

Berk's jaw clenches. "Not. Funny." He is coughing. Maybe I overdid it.

Rhen has shears and is removing the portion of Berk's suit that covers his injury. I don't mean to but I gasp. The wounds are deep. And they are long, like the wolf sank its fangs as far down as it could and then pulled.

Berk looks at Rhen. "What do you think?"

"There is a great deal of blood. But I don't think the animals punctured a vital artery."

Rhen places small medical capsules in each of the puncture sites. Berk screams and I grab his hand in both of mine.

"This will clean out the wound and stop the bleeding," Rhen explains.

Berk tries to answer but he can't speak. He is too weak, in too much pain.

I turn away. It isn't the blood that keeps me from being able to watch; it is the knowledge that this—all of this—is my fault. I walk away from Berk, curl up on my sleeping platform, and pull the covering over my head.

Berk is dying. And I cannot watch that happen.

CHAPTER FOUR

Thalli."

I hear Rhen, but I'm not sure how. She is so far away. I am in our cube in Pod C, and she is . . . outside?

"Thalli, open your eyes."

I open them, but all I see is white. Then I remember—I am in the chamber. "Berk!"

"He's going to be all right." Rhen lays my head back down. "You need to eat something."

I fell asleep. I turn my head. Berk is on the other side of the chamber. He is sleeping. I watch his chest rise and fall, rise and fall, making sure he really is alive.

Rhen hands me a piece of bread and a container of juice. I lift myself—slowly—and eat, keeping my eyes on Berk all the time.

"We're going to have to make some changes." Logical Rhen is in control. Of course. Always ready with a plan. "The animals will come back."

"Wolves."

"What?"

I take a sip of my juice. "They are wolves, probably mutated by the radiation. But I recognize them from one of my lessons."

"So you actually *did* study?"

I almost choke on my bread. Rhen is never anything but logical, normal. All facts. I can't believe she would even choose to be lighthearted right now. "Yes. And they are dangerous."

"I can see that." Rhen glances at Berk. Her eyes stay on him. Like mine do. "What are we going to do to prevent another attack?"

"Stay here when we're on the ground, and stay well aboveground when we're on the transport."

"But how will we cook our food?" Rhen turns her bread in her hands. "How will we keep the wolves from waiting outside the chamber?"

"The siren frightens them. One of us could stay on the transport while we're cooking the food."

"What about when we exit the chamber?"

There are no windows in the chamber. No cameras to show us what is happening outside. Rhen is right. If the wolves are waiting outside, we wouldn't have time to get to the transport and sound the siren. Unless . . . "We keep the transport in here with us."

Rhen's eyes widen. "Where?"

"We don't use our sleeping platforms, you and I." The transport is just a little larger than our two platforms put together. "We can sleep on it. Then we can activate the siren before we open the chamber."

"Of course." Rhen rubs her temples. "I should have thought of that."

"Is John asleep?" In my concern for Berk, I hadn't even thought of John. I turn to see him on his knees on the floor beside his bed, his head cradled in his arms.

"I don't think so." Rhen's gaze flits from John to Berk. "He's praying."

"Praying?"

"Talking to the Designer." I have spoken to Rhen about the Designer before. John has too, but she doesn't like to discuss him.

Rhen nods. "He told me he was doing that earlier. When Berk was being attacked."

I think of Berk's escape from the wolves. How did I know to find the siren panel? Why would there even be a siren panel on a transport? Did the Designer plan even that for us? John always says the Designer is working all things together for our good. But if that is true, why wouldn't he have kept the wolves from attacking us in the first place?

John looks up. "I was thanking him for Berk's deliverance."

Rhen bites her lip, looks at Berk, and nods again. "And how are you feeling, John?"

"Full of hope, Rhen." John stands slowly. Pain clouds his eyes but his smile never fades. "Full of hope."

"Those wolves..." Even with our plan to keep the transport in here, I am worried. What if they aren't the only animals that survived? What if the pockets of surviving humans have been mutated as well?

"Those wolves are living on the earth." John eases himself down on his sleeping platform. "And you were breathing on your own out there. Both are good signs."

"But those wolves are mutated." I breathe in a clean lungful of air. "What if I become mutated too?"

"The wolves have adapted to life here, yes." John dips his head slightly. "But their appearance has more to do with their diet and lifestyle than mutations. Given proper food and water, they would likely look just like their predecessors. The point is—they are living. Even here, there must be some food and some water."

"John is correct." Rhen's hand is on Berk's wrist. She is checking his pulse, but it seems so much more personal, so tender. I want to be the one caring for him, touching him. But Rhen knows more about medicine than I.

"If the air were toxic, you would have shown signs by now," Rhen says. "But you're fine. The air might still have traces of radiation, but it is no longer saturated with it."

"So we can remove our helmets as we travel?" John's eyes no longer reflect pain. They are light and alive.

"I don't think that is a good idea yet." Rhen removes her hand from Berk's wrist. Finally. But she is still looking at him. "We don't know how much exposure is too much. We are safer wearing the helmets until we can test it."

"Why can't we just test it now?" I agree with John— traveling without the weight of the helmets is appealing.

Rhen moves away from Berk and lowers her voice. "Because that is Berk's area, and we can't force him to do too much too soon. His injuries are severe. It will take time for him to recuperate from the blood loss. And there is still danger of infection in his leg. The wounds are very deep."

"I thought you medicated that."

"I did." Rhen rubs her temples. "But this isn't like an injury in the State. I don't know what was in the animal's saliva. And our bodies are not equipped to fight off the diseases they may carry."

"What are you saying?" My heart feels like it is in my throat, choking me.

"She is saying that this may kill me." Berk's voice sounds unused, like a trombone with a battered horn. He clears his throat, his green eyes barely open. "But it won't. I won't let it. I did not escape the State and the Scientists to be destroyed by a ragged bunch of wolves."

John walks over to Berk and lays his gnarled hand on Berk's shoulder. "One of the names for the Designer is the Great Physician. So let us appeal to him now, together."

Rhen and I walk to Berk and we each grab one of his hands. I look at Berk's hand in Rhen's and it makes my stomach ache. I struggle to even hear John's words.

"Thank you, Father, for your protection . . ."

Something is happening between Berk and Rhen. I see it in how they look at each other, how Rhen's eyes soften when she speaks to him. I cannot stop it. But it is making my heart break.

"Heal him . . ."

I lift my eyes to see Rhen's face. She is crying. Rhen is supposed to be normal. She never cries. Yet there she is, holding Berk's hand, crying over him. I understand loving Berk. Even when I was angry with him, I felt it. But I don't want anyone else to feel it. I want Berk to myself.

"You are powerful. You have healed the blind and raised the dead . . ."

I want to be praying for Berk. I should be praying for Berk. But all I can think of is that I'm losing Berk. Not to the jaws of a wolf, but to my best friend.

"But in all things, Father, we submit our will to yours. Amen."

CHAPTER FIVE

I need my violin.

We have been traveling for six days. We were supposed to arrive at the colony by tomorrow. But in four days, nothing has changed. No vegetation, no water, nothing. The only good that happened is that after two days of checking the air, Berk gave us permission to remove our helmets. We are far enough away from the contaminated air that we no longer need them.

Twice more, the wolves came. We were able to use the siren to scare them away, but they seemed less frightened of it each time. And more have come each time. Even if there were human survivors, wouldn't they be killed by these predators? I cannot help but think we are traveling closer to death with every mile.

Berk is still weak. Rhen is still caring for him. They are together all the time. She has to tend to his wounds, check his vital signs. I am left to do the cooking and the watching. John tries to talk to me, but I do not want to talk. The only thing in my mind is a feeling I can't describe, but it's not good. Anger boils in me the way our food boils as it is being prepared.

I could play this feeling if I had my violin. But I don't. I am desperate, though. So I excuse myself, take the transport away from the chamber—high enough that if the wolves came, I would be safe—and imagine the violin is in my arms. I hum the notes. It is not the same, but I have to do something, play something, or I fear everything in my mind and my heart will erupt out of my mouth.

And Berk would likely feel guilty if that happened, taxing his already compromised system. I cannot be that selfish. He needs to recover. His being alive is more important than his loving me.

But that thought makes a piece of my heart feel like it has fallen off onto the ashy ground below.

I look down and see the chamber being dismantled. I am hesitant to ask Berk if we are on schedule to arrive at the colony tomorrow. Part of me is frightened at the prospect. Another part is desperate for other people. But the most honest part wants to just forget all this and turn myself back in to the State. And maybe, once I know the other three are settled and all right, I'll do that. Maybe if I return, they will be safe.

"Thalli." Rhen is calling. It is time to begin today's journey.

I lower the transport. Berk limps aboard. He is still pale,

weak, sleeping most of the time. But his leg seems to be healing. Whatever diseases the wolves may have had were destroyed by Rhen's medical capsules. Or John's prayer. I do not know which.

"We are not far." Berk sounds so close, yet he feels so far away. Farther than he has ever felt. The green grid pops on the screen in front of my eyes. The orange dots are bigger. "We will arrive tomorrow. Continue on the same course."

Rhen nods at me, and then she presses a button that allows her to communicate with Berk alone. John stands across from me, and I move the transport up and toward those orange dots. I want to look behind me, at Rhen and Berk. I want to hear what they are discussing. But we must all wear the helmets to help us navigate. And the helmets create an impenetrable barrier.

The transport makes a sudden dip. I must have accidentally touched the wrong panel. I press the panel to move us forward, but it dips again.

"What is wrong?" Rhen asks.

"I don't know." We are dipping faster now. We will hit the ground hard if I can't stop this.

"Try the yellow panel." Berk tries to stand, but the transport dips once again and he is thrown to the floor. Rhen's quick reflexes save him from toppling over the side of the transport onto the ashy ground.

I press my finger onto the yellow panel. Nothing. I slam it as hard as I can, using my thumb, index finger, and two fingers together. Nothing. We are going to crash.

"Relax your muscles," Rhen orders. "There is less chance of injury if we are relaxed."

The idea is ridiculous. Every part of me wants to tighten,

but I will my muscles to disregard those signals. I remain as limp as I can.

"Stay where you are," Rhen shouts. "Try to land it flat. We don't want the transport to flip."

I try to relax but maintain my position. I look at Berk, who is barely conscious. The transport careens toward the ground. I cannot keep its front end from tilting downward.

"Move to the back," I shout. "We need more weight in the back."

We are seconds away from impact. I do not have time to look and see if the others moved, but the transport makes a slight shift. Not enough, though. We hit the ground hard, my end first, then the other.

I am thrown off, my helmet falls off as I tumble several feet away from where we landed. My mouth and eyes are full of dirt. I am coughing and crying, trying to see the others but unable to make anything out.

"Thalli." Rhen sounds so far away. "Call out if you can hear me."

I try to speak, but I can only cough. The dust feels like it has taken up residence in my throat.

"It's okay," Rhen calls out. "I see you. Berk?"

I rub my eyes harder. Where is he? "On the transport." Berk wrapped himself around the column. Smart. He is safe.

"John?"

I sit up, look around. John is not near me. He is not on the transport with Berk.

"John." Fear creeps into Rhen's voice. I feel it too. John is not answering. I stand. My vision is blurry. But not so blurry I don't see the body of an old man lying motionless in the dust.

CHAPTER SIX

R hen is running to John. I follow, tripping over some larger pieces of earth. I right myself and keep going. John cannot be dead.

Rhen falls to the ground next to him and lays her head on his chest. I stand above them, frozen. It seems as if hours pass. Rhen doesn't move. John's face reminds me of another face—Dr. Spires. I saw him dead on the ground outside Pod C, so many months ago. The slack jaw, the pale skin. The horrible sensation in the recesses of my stomach. It all feels exactly the same.

"I hear a heartbeat." Rhen sits up. "But it is faint."

I let out a breath I didn't know I was holding.

"John, can you hear me?" Rhen shakes the old man, but he doesn't stir. His head falls to the side. The dust around his mouth barely moves. "We need to get him inside the chamber."

Berk stands and tries to limp toward the chamber's container, but by the look on his face, he is in pain. "Stay there, Berk. I can do it."

Berk starts to speak, but Rhen interrupts. "We need you completely healed, Berk. You can't do that if you don't rest. Thalli can set up the chamber."

He sits back down, like an obedient child given a command by a Monitor. I walk toward the chamber. It must have been the first to fall off the transport because it is several feet behind us. I have to pull hard to lift it—the speed at which it fell caused it to be partially buried in the ground.

I hope the chamber hasn't been damaged. I cannot tell from the outside. If we lose this, there is nothing to keep us safe from the wolves or any other creatures that might be lurking. I press the blue panel, and the chamber unpacks itself. It is dirty but unharmed.

I wish I could say the same about John.

"Will he be all right?" I look at Rhen, who is assessing John's condition.

"I believe he has suffered a concussion." Rhen motions for me to lift his feet. She is by his shoulders. Together, we carry him to the chamber and gently lay him on a sleeping platform.

"Will he be all right?"

"I am not sure," Rhen says after a lengthy pause. "He is very old. Nothing I studied prepared me to understand the way a body works at this age."

"We should help Berk."

"I will help him. You stay here with John. If he regains consciousness, we need to make sure he stays awake."

Rhen assumes responsibility for Berk. She assumes that he needs *her*, not me. And this time it isn't for medical reasons. If it were that, then Rhen would stay behind here with John. But she chose Berk. She wants to be the one who helps him walk back. She wants to make sure he's all right. To touch him and talk to him and care for him.

I swallow past a lump in my throat and try to calm myself. To relax my emotions the way I relaxed my muscles on the transport. I need to focus on John and not think about Rhen and Berk.

John's eyelids move, but they don't open. I bend down close to him and place my hands on the sides of his face, his white beard poking up between my fingers. "John. Wake up. Please wake up."

His eyelids move again, and I will him to open them, to be all right. A moan escapes John's mouth.

"You're okay, John." I pull away, giving him space but keeping my eyes on his. "The transport fell. You were thrown off."

I can't think of anything else to say. He won't open his eyes, and I can't let him go back to sleep. The only other thing I can think of right now is Rhen and Berk, and I don't want to talk to him about that.

"John." His eyelids stop moving. I have to speak, to keep him awake. "Rhen is with Berk. I think she has feelings for him. But I don't want her to have feelings. It makes me . . . I don't know. Angry. Sad."

"Jealous." John's voice sounds like a muted saxophone.

"You're awake." I am so relieved, I barely register what he has said. John opens his eyes. I can tell just that takes great effort.

"You're jealous." He lifts his bushy eyebrows.

"What?"

"That feeling is jealousy."

We don't have time to discuss it because Berk limps in—aided by Rhen. Her arm is around his shoulders, his arm is looped around her waist. This . . . jealousy is strong. I fight it and try to focus on John. "He's awake."

"Excellent." Rhen helps Berk to his sleeping platform and then walks over to assess John. She looks into his eyes, takes his pulse, asks him questions.

I barely hear any of them. I am trying to look at Berk without him noticing. He seems to be looking at John. But maybe he's also looking at Rhen. And why wouldn't he? Blond hair, blue eyes, always in control of her emotions, always knowing what to do. Unlike me—an anomaly who is only alive because these two saved me from the death I deserved because I couldn't keep my emotions in check.

Rhen completes her examination. "I think he will make a full recovery. But we need to keep him awake for the next few hours."

"That's fine." Berk rises, limps over to us, then sits on the edge of John's sleeping platform. "We have plenty to talk about."

For the first time, the reality of what just happened hit me—we have no transport. We are still forty miles away from our destination with half our party unable to travel without assistance. We were on schedule to arrive tomorrow, but that was on the transport. Forty miles on foot with John and Berk could take weeks. We don't have enough food for weeks.

Have we survived a crash, only to die of starvation? Or worse?

CHAPTER SEVEN

The transport is not receiving enough energy." Berk insisted that we bring the transport inside the chamber so he could investigate the cause of yesterday's crash. It is dirty and damaged, causing the inside of the chamber to look more like the outside. Nothing is clean aboveground. "It is equipped to run using solar power, but the sun has been hidden behind clouds since we left."

"But the whole State runs on solar power." There must have been clouds over the State for as many days as there have been clouds over us. "The transport hardly needs anything compared to the State."

"We had power outages," Berk reminds me.

I think of the times he took advantage of those outages to see me, and I am sad. Times when he held me and talked to me, when he could not wait to be alone with me. Are those days lost forever?

Berk looks at me. He is focused on the task, not lost in memories of the past. "But we also had artificial light that helped power the State."

"There are seasons of sunlight and seasons of cloudiness." Rhen looks at her learning pad. "We left during a cloudy season."

"When will that change?"

Rhen doesn't look up from her pad. "I can't determine. It could be weeks."

We don't have weeks. We all know that, but no one wants to say it.

"We should pray."

John needs to stay awake, so I don't argue with him. But the transport crashed, and I doubt if it will work even if the sun does come out.

Berk and Rhen close their eyes when John does. I cannot. I watch them, doubt filling my heart. Why would the Designer allow us to crash? Why let us escape and then leave us to die here? Why have me fall in love with Berk only to have Berk fall in love with Rhen? Or maybe John is wrong and the Designer really isn't in control of everything. Maybe his power is limited.

John finishes his prayer, and Rhen leans closer to him. "You really believe your God will help us?"

"I am certain of it, my dear."

"Why?"

"I have known him for many years." John speaks softly but we all listen. As upset as I am, I still want to hear his answer, to glean some of his confidence. "I hear his voice in the words I have memorized. His words. They are true. They have always been true. I also hear him when he speaks to my heart. And he is speaking now. We will arrive at our destination. Our promised land."

I have heard God speak to my heart. Through music. I heard him when I played "Jesu, Joy of Man's Desiring." He showed me who he was, even though I did not know it at first. I heard him when I played the music I wrote in the performance pod. I want to hear him again. I wonder if I can, without an instrument. Is it only through music that I can talk to him, that I can hear him? But out here, in this desolate space, there is no music. I feel as dry as the earth.

We begin to plan how we will travel. *Rhen* plans how we will travel. Rhen will help Berk and I will help John. I want to argue, to shout that I want to be with Berk. I want Berk to say he wants me. But neither of us says anything, and my heart aches even more than it did before.

We will walk only as long as the two men can go. They must tell us when they are too tired or hurt to continue. Then we will set up the chamber and rest. I will carry the chamber on my back—wrapped around me with a bed covering. Rhen will carry the transport in the same way, watching the skies to see if the sun will come out and we can recharge it. If it still works.

By the end of our eighth day walking, every muscle in my body hurts. John is still weak, and he leans heavily on me. The chamber isn't heavy, but it is large and balancing it and John is hard. I have to stop often to readjust the pack. We are being careful with what little food and water we have remaining, and I am constantly hungry, my mouth dry. No wolves have approached us yet, but the elements will surely kill us, even if the wolves are gone.

Rhen and Berk walk ahead of us, always deep in conversation. They rarely look back at us. I purposefully lag behind. I don't want to walk beside them listening in on what I am sure are private conversations.

"Did I ever tell you about Chris?" John pushes his shoulder into mine.

"Chris?"

"He was a boy who attended the same college as Amy and me." John's voice always gets tender when he speaks of his wife. Like a saxophone playing a slow melody. "He was good looking, popular, ended up being a preacher. A pretty famous one, at that. We all knew he was something special. And he had his eye on my Amy."

When John speaks about the past, he uses so many words I do not know, and I sometimes have to ask him to translate. But while I may not know all the words, I understand what he is saying. "He loved her?"

John laughs and runs his hand down my hair. "I don't think Chris loved Amy, but he liked her. And who could blame him? She was the prettiest girl who ever was, and her inside—her character—was even more beautiful than her outside."

My gaze drifts to Rhen. The same could be said of her. She is calm, intelligent, and she always knows the right thing to do.

"I couldn't stand it when I saw Amy and Chris talking." John sighs. "One time I saw them outside the student center, sitting at a picnic table just laughing away. I got so mad, I wanted to hit him."

I cannot imagine John angry. "Why?"

"I was jealous." John stops and forces me to look into his eyes. "I loved Amy so much that it made me mad to think of any other guy stealing her attention away from me. The thought that she might choose another guy over me . . . well, that just about killed me."

"I understand." I do not want to hit Rhen, but I am jealous. And angry. But more than anything, I am sad. I want Berk's attention. I want to talk with him. I want things to be the way they were before, when we were in the State. When he wanted to be with me.

"God had a lesson for me in that, though," John says. "A lesson I think he is trying to teach you too."

"A lesson?"

"Romantic love is a beautiful thing, but not when it replaces divine love."

I turn away from John and start walking again.

John steps beside me, quiet for a minute, then continues. "I remember standing on the grass, looking at Chris and Amy, and thinking, 'I have made her an idol.' I allowed what was meant to be beautiful to be changed into something ugly."

"What did you do?"

"I walked back to the dorm room, got on my knees, and repented. I thanked God for allowing me to see my sin for what it was, and I surrendered to his will for my life. No matter what that was."

"And you got Amy back."

"That wasn't the point of the story." John takes my hand in

his age-worn hand. "You need a change in perspective, Thalli, not a change in circumstance. Joy comes from the Designer alone. Humans, even the best humans, are flawed. We cannot meet each other's needs completely. We were not designed to do that. We were created to be in relationship with the Designer. In him, we find true joy and peace. We find freedom in loving him and being loved by him. When we look to others to fill that hole, we find ourselves empty."

I do feel empty. Not just empty, but used and discarded. I wish again that I had my violin, that I could communicate with the Designer so he felt nearer. I do not feel his love. I do not feel Berk's love. I feel fear and jealousy and hopelessness. I gaze up into the sky. Still covered with clouds, the ground still gray. It would have been better to have stayed in the State. I was closer to God when I faced annihilation than I am out here.

I look at John and see his face change. I assume he is thinking of Amy again, preparing to tell me the rest of the story. But his eyes are focused on something in the distance. Something that brings him joy. I follow his gaze and see a huge animal lumbering toward us. I cannot even make out what type of animal it is, it moves so fast. But John knows. He is laughing. He releases my hand and moves faster than I have seen him move in days.

I cannot look at the animal anymore. I am chasing John. Surely, the last of his sanity just departed.

CHAPTER EIGHT

ood boy." John allows the animal's mouth to cover his face. He is delirious. I try to pull the animal off the old man, but I cannot. John's arms are actually around it. He is holding on to it. "Oh, how I have missed the affection of a dog."

"A dog?" I recall learning about dogs. They were revered by the ancients, allowed to live in homes, and called "pets." John sits up, rubbing the dog's face with his hands, scratching behind the animal's ears. The huge tail waves back and forth. Its saliva-filled tongue hangs out. The animal actually looks happy.

"I had one just like this." John rubs the dog's back with his palm. "A black Lab. Beautiful creature. And this one is obviously well taken care of."

Berk's eyes brighten. "Well taken care of? So there are people here?"

"Yes." John smiles. "And if my friend is any indication, they are good people."

"What makes you think that?" Rhen joins us, her arm still through Berk's.

"Look at his coat." John smooths down the fur on the dog's back. Shiny. "He is brushed often and fed well. And he is friendly—not mistreated or frightened. Labs are kind dogs anyway. But this one—" John laughs as the dog licks his face. "He is especially friendly."

"We're almost there?" Hope fills my heart, pushing aside all other feelings.

"Most certainly." John begins to ease to his feet. "Our friend here will show us the way. Won't you, boy?"

I look at Rhen. She is frozen in place. "What if the people aren't friendly to us?"

"What?" John places a hand on my shoulder to steady himself as he stands.

"We don't know anything about them." Rhen looks to Berk. "We could be walking into a trap."

That same thought entered my mind. We know nothing about this settlement. We know nothing about whether or not they have been affected by the radiation, nothing about how they view foreigners. Nothing about their technology or their way of life or their values.

John gives a slow nod. "This is where we simply have to trust the Designer."

"Shouldn't we plan for an attack, just in case?" The thought of just walking up to a settlement of people we know nothing about makes my heart race.

"If they plan to harm us, there is no way for us to stop them." Berk's voice is soft but sure. "We need to go on. We will run out of food soon, and both John and I need to rest."

Berk is still so pale. He is right. But that fact doesn't make the possibilities any less frightening.

The dog is now running back in the direction he came from. We watch him run off. John lets out an earsplitting whistle and the dog returns, his tongue out, that happy look on his face.

"Slow down, boy." John's laugh makes him sound years younger. The way I imagine he sounded before the War stripped him of everything. "We don't move as quickly as you do."

We walk along, though John is moving faster, and he and I lead the way. Actually, the dog is leading the way. John tells me about his dog, and how Duke would sleep at the foot of Amy's and his bed. How John would find Duke's long black hairs on his clothes. He speaks of going to the beach with Duke and throwing something called a Frisbee that the dog would catch and bring back to him. A game called "fetch" that would go on for hours, until John was tired and needed to rest. He speaks of his son, Dr. Turner, and how Duke was a puppy when his son left home for college. The dog kept John and Amy company when their house was no longer filled with the sounds of children.

"I remember once—" John stops so quickly we almost fall. I am still moving; he is as still as a pod.

"What?" I look in the direction he is staring, and the land-scape is changing. The ground is raised ahead of us, round like a pod but gray on the side facing us. At the top, however, it is not gray. It appears to be green. Green like the grass that grows in our recreation field. But this is not a recreation area created by Scientists. This is actual grass, untouched by the War. Undeniable proof that not all of the earth was destroyed.

"We're close." John pulls me along, oblivious to his injuries. "Come. Come."

It takes us several minutes. The land is a hill—I remember this from when I was in Progress. But Progress was a simulation of life aboveground, and this is not. This is real. The effort to walk up the hill is taxing to John, but a smile never leaves his face.

When we arrive at the top, he falls to his knees, his face buried in a tall patch of grass. "Thank you, thank you, thank you."

I move away, not wanting to intrude on John's moment with the Designer.

Rhen and Berk are almost at the top. Rhen is practically dragging Berk. I run down to them, step to Berk's other side, and help Rhen carry him up. When we arrive, John is standing. He points down the hill.

"Look." He wipes the tears from his eyes. "We have arrived."

CHAPTER NINE

We can see the settlement in the distance. There are pods and recreation fields and other animals, different from the dog but seemingly calm. Not like the wolves we encountered. The hope I have begun to feel grows.

"We are still far away." Rhen surveys the settlement.

"Then let us begin now." John puts his arm through mine and urges me down the hill. "Look—a pond."

John releases my arm and moves quicker than I have ever seen him move. I am worried he will fall, causing further injury to himself, so I chase after him. The terrain changes as we go down the hill, closer to the pond. A strange wind blows past me, cool and moist, but I do not have time to consider what that means. John is running directly to the water.

"John, no!" He doesn't know what's in that water.

But the huge dog jumps in and John follows right behind, his whole body going underneath. The water is so brown, I cannot see John. I cannot swim. In Progress, I went into a lake. But I did not go under. John is in there and he is not coming up. Rhen and Berk are still far behind. I stand at the edge of the pond, my heart pounding a staccato rhythm.

"Come on in." John is suddenly in the center of the pond. How he got there, I have no idea, but there he is, the dog right beside him, going in circles around John, who is now floating on his back. "The water is fine."

John gulps a mouthful of water and spits it up into the air. It makes an arc and then splashes beside him. The dog lunges for it and goes under, then back up. My fear eases. John is all right. He is beyond all right. Joy that I have never seen before shines from his face. Peace, I have seen. But this is different . . . He is home.

I take a step toward the pond. The closer I get, the moister the ground beneath my feet becomes. I pull off my shoes and allow my feet to plunge deeper into the soil. It feels strangely cool. So different from the ashy dust we have covering every inch of our bodies. This feels almost clean. My feet are sinking into the ground, and I wiggle my toes. The sensation causes me to laugh. I can't help myself.

"It is good to hear you laugh." Berk is behind me, his breath hot on my neck. I want to turn around, to hold him, feel his heart beating. But I cannot. I should not. He is probably just speaking as a friend. Nothing more.

"Is he safe?" Rhen is next to Berk. Berk steps back, and I no longer feel his breath.

"Yes, I am safe," John calls out. "I'm swimming. Join me."

Rhen's and Berk's faces mirror what I'm feeling. We will not go into that filthy pond.

John must be tossing the water in our direction because I feel it on my head. Just a few drops at first, but then more. So much more that I am certain it cannot be John's doing. I look around, afraid someone else is here, mocking us, flinging water at us. Then John moves toward us, his face lifted toward the sky.

"Rain!" John's arms are spread out in front of him. His shirt and pants are dripping with pond water as he stands, smiling. I look up and notice water all around us. It is not being tossed. It is falling from the sky.

"Rain." Rhen lifts her palm and the drops of water fall on her skin.

We learned about rain. It is part of the weather patterns that were on earth. We learned about the process of evaporation and condensation. But we did not see it. Our greenhouses had moisture imbedded in the soil. The Botanists created ways to irrigate everything without wasting water. We were taught that on earth, people splashed water around, that it ran haphazardly throughout the streets. We could not be so careless. Our water supply had to go through years of processing to become viable.

But this is not the State, and this is not a waste. It is pure water, carelessly dropping on everything and everyone. Drops splash into the pond, creating ribbons of movement all around it. It is beautiful.

I close my eyes and feel the drops run down my face, my

neck, soaking my shirt. The ground seems to smell sweeter, the air feels cooler. We had showers in the pods, but they were nothing like this. Quick rinses with fast-flowing water coming out in a steady stream. This feels more like a caress.

All of us are silent in the face of the rain. It is amazing. Breathtaking. I want to share this moment with Berk, to feel him near me again. I want to apologize, to start over. I turn to see him and find he is once again with Rhen. Talking with her, standing near her, sharing *our* moment with her.

I am not sure if it's the rain or my tears I feel rolling down my cheeks.

CHAPTER TEN

hear something." Rhen steps away from Berk, her gaze on the horizon. The village is close. We can see it in the distance. Fear creeps back into my heart—fear of what the people might be like, what dangers might be waiting for us.

"What is that?" I place my hands over my eyes. The sun is bright now, and its glare from the pond is almost blinding. The noise is getting louder, a pounding with a metallic clanging and screeching. An odd combination of sounds. I hear the dog barking and another animal sound. It seems to be attached to whatever is pounding, so it is a large animal. I try to remember my zoology lessons and once again find myself frustrated at not having paid attention.

"Horses."

Of course Rhen would know. We all stand and watch as two horses—now I remember reading about them—pull a long metal box on wheels toward us. The box looks ancient and has holes in it that look like they were made by thousands of tiny animals taking small bites out of the metal. The spaces around the holes are a sick shade of brown. Along the side of the box are letters: *D-O* then a huge hole and *G-E*.

"Ingenius." John claps his hands as the contraption gets closer. "A horse-drawn truck. Only in Texas."

I don't recall the word *truck*, but I cannot bother with that now. My gaze is on the man sitting behind the horses. He appears to be almost as old as John, but with no hair on his head and a long beard that is equal parts silver and black. He is holding two long ropes attached to a mechanism that keeps the horses together. He stops several feet from us and for long moments, none of us says a word.

The old man lowers himself from the truck, still holding on to the ropes. His eyes never leave us. He seems suspicious. I suppose I cannot blame him. I am suspicious as well.

"We have escaped from an underground compound in Colorado." John finally breaks the silence.

The old man, still clutching the ropes, takes one step forward. "Colorado is a long way away."

"We had a transport." John motions to the spot where we left it soaking in the sun's rays. "It broke down, but we think it might work again with a little more solar power."

"Look, we're simple folks." The man stays rooted in place, his eyes tiny slits. "And we like it that way."

The man speaks differently than we do. His vowels are soft

and his words take longer to come out than ours. I understand him, but it is difficult. What does he think of how we speak? We must look strange to him. Even though we are wet and dirty, our clothes are very different from his. We all wear the white suits of the State. His clothes are faded but colorful, his pants a dingy blue and his shirt a combination of several colors in a variety of patterns. His shoes are caked with dirt, but even if they were clean, I am fairly certain they would still be the color of the ground beside the pond.

"We are homeless," John says. "We are not looking to change your way of life, but we would like to join you. We are almost out of food."

"And they are hurt." I cannot remain silent any longer. "John fell, and Berk was attacked by wolves. Do you have a Medical Specialist?"

"We have a healer." The man motions for us to climb in the back of his truck. "But before you see her, you need to see the Scientists."

CHAPTER ELEVEN

My heart plunges. The Scientists? They found us? Followed us here? Have they been tracking us all along? Watching as we traveled, laughing as we crashed? The four of us are silent as the truck turns around and the horses point us toward the village. The old man refuses to say any more. When we ask him about the Scientists, he just shrugs and says, "You'll see."

I have led my friends to their deaths. I want to turn us back around, to push the old man down and see if we can make the sixty miles to the next village. Maybe they will protect us from the Scientists.

I look at the old man, and I know I cannot do that. And if

the Scientists made it to this village ahead of us, then they will surely be able to follow us to the next. I try to think about something else, anything to keep the images of Berk, Rhen, and John being annihilated from playing in my mind.

"What are those?" I point to a group of animals about the size of the horses. They are of varying colors of brown and white, wider than the horses, their thick necks bent to eat grass.

"Cows." John rubs his long white beard. "Dairy cows, used for getting milk and cream and butter and cheese."

"Ancient foods?" Rhen does not hide her disgust.

The foods in the State are all grown in the greenhouses or manufactured in the labs to be of optimal nutritional value. We were told the ancients ate animals and drank their secretions and that the diseases that resulted from that practice killed many. I am a little nauseous at the thought of it.

"I hope they have some beef cattle in there." John cranes his neck to see. "What I wouldn't give to have a juicy steak."

"We got 'em." The driver turns to look at John. "Over in the west pasture. What did they feed you folks up there?"

"You don't want to know." John and the grizzled driver share a laugh.

Beyond the fence that holds the dairy cattle, I see trees. Many trees, all together. "Are those oranges?"

"They sure are." John smiles. "I didn't realize Texas grew oranges. We had huge orange groves in California. A buddy of mine managed one of the largest, way down south. It was a lot of work, but they'd produce thousands and thousands of oranges every year. We used to take the kids down after he harvested. They did it with machines, but the machines missed some. So old Charlie would let us come with big baskets and take as many as we could eat. The kids would eat five or six just on the ride home, then we'd squeeze them into the best orange juice you've ever tasted. And Amy—" John laughs. "Amy could make all kinds of things with the leftovers. Oranges with chicken, with fish, in smoothies and cakes and muffins. She was quite a cook."

"That sounds wonderful." Such culinary variety was not part of life in the State.

"It was."

The driver glances at John. "Where in California you from?"

"Just west of San Diego."

"That was beautiful country."

John nods. "Sure was."

"My parents were from Sacramento." The driver turns to face John. "We used to drive up there every summer to visit my grandparents. We always stopped in San Diego to visit the zoo."

"We had season passes when the kids were little." John smiles.

The driver turns back around, but he has a smile on his face. I try to imagine what this world was like before the War, when people could travel hundreds of miles and see cities all along the way, not just long stretches of dust-covered nothing-ness. A place filled with families and zoos and friends. I can't fathom that world. It is strange that it existed just four decades ago, that John still remembers it so clearly.

"Look at the pods." Berk points to the structures so differ-ent from ones in the State that they can hardly be classified as pods.

From a distance they looked a little different. Not white, but I expected that. I saw pods in Progress, and even though they weren't real, they were modeled after the images of ancient dwellings we saw on our learning pads. But even those did not look like these. The exteriors are made from trees, cut into long pieces and fit together. Remnants of ancient homes are scattered around, obviously vacant and picked through.

John must see the questions in my eyes because he places his hand over mine. "All the homes before the War were dependent on technology. In that way, they were no different than the State. My guess is that this town survived damage from the War, but the technology was wiped out all around the globe. Easier to build something new than to try to fix the old."

The driver turns around. His voice has an edge to it, although I don't understand why. "We have a simple way of life here, and that's how we like it. If you want something else, I suggest you head on over to Athens."

John leans toward the driver. "Please excuse me if I sounded critical. I think you have a fine town, and we are grateful for your hospitality."

The driver grunts but seems to relax in his seat. The distractions of the cows and the trees are gone, replaced again by a suffocating fear. We are almost there. Almost to where the Scientists are waiting for us. My mind races with the possibilities as the truck slows.

We are in front of a huge structure. This is different from the pods. It is made from cement—like the ends of the State. It is massive, with holes in the front I assume were once windows.

John chuckles beside me. An odd sound at a time like this. "An old Walmart."

"What?"

But he doesn't have time to respond because out of the

structure come two older, distinguished people, a man and a woman. The man has reddish hair sprinkled with white. His fair skin is slightly wrinkled. He is thin but appears healthy. The woman has dark hair, curly but short. Her skin is a light brown—similar to my podmate Asta, who was annihilated when we were nine. The woman appears to be the same age as the man, a little heavier with fewer wrinkles and no white hair.

The driver motions to the couple. "These are the Scientists."

I let out a loud exhale, relief replacing fear. These are not State Scientists. They do not appear to have intentions to kill us. They look curious, not angry.

"Where did you come from?"

Berk eases himself out of the truck to face the Scientists. "We are from the State. We were scheduled to be annihilated, so we escaped."

The woman's eyes narrow. "How did you escape?"

Berk explains his plan—stealing decontamination suits and food and a transport and a chamber, then looking up the map.

"And how do you know you aren't being followed?" The man raises his eyebrows.

"We don't know for sure," Berk explains. "But we have been traveling for almost two weeks. If they were to come after us, they would have done so by now."

"So the State still exists." The man looks at the woman, and something unspoken passes between them.

"You know about the State?" I ask. With no technology, how could they possibly be aware the State even exists?

The woman steps forward and takes a deep breath. "We escaped from the State too."

CHAPTER TWELVE

The Scientists have ushered us into their pod. They know we have questions, but they want to ask us their questions first. They fill a table with food as they ask, and we have no choice but to answer. Actually, Berk is talking while the rest of us are eating. As curious as I am, I am even hungrier.

John devours the strange foods. I cannot bring myself to try the meat or cheese, but I do eat the fruit and vegetables. I even manage to taste what they call "dip" on a slice of carrot. It is different. A creamy texture I am sure I don't want to know the source of. But I might try it again. Later.

"How are they accounting for the oxygen issue?" The woman is very concerned with the oxygen in the State.

I have heard variations of this question several times now. But I don't hear Berk's answer. I don't want to think about the State, don't want to talk about the State. I want to forget it, to believe we're in a place where we are all safe.

This building is odd. It was obviously once one gigantic pod, but now it is divided into several pods. We are in a section like a living area, with places to sit and a kitchen. I wander out the door to the next section. It is larger—about the size of the music chamber in the State. There are at least two dozen chairs with desks. Some smaller than others. Bookshelves line the walls.

I have never seen a real book, just pictures of them on my learning pad. They look beautiful, all different colors and sizes. They are arranged alphabetically by author. I want to read one. We were taught that stories were for ancients because they could not deal with reality. We were conditioned to understand facts and not require any type of escape. But I escaped through music. And I loved it. I have always wondered if stories would be the same.

I pick up a book by someone with a last name of Dickens. The book feels as if it could fall apart in my hands. The pages are brittle and yellow, and someone has written all along the sides of the pages and underlined sentences. We would never be allowed to do that in the State. And there are so many words. Too many. We were taught that communication should always be direct. Never use five words when one will suffice. Obviously this Dickens did not receive that same instruction.

"Thalli."

Rhen's voice surprises me, and I slam the book closed. "Yes. Of course. I am coming." I am embarrassed to have been caught in here. Will Rhen and Berk laugh about me together when they are alone? The thought makes me sad. I should be thankful—we are here in this village, and the people seem friendly. They have food and pods. My friends are safe. But I still miss Berk.

John, Berk, and the Scientists are sitting on the couches in the living area. Rhen and I sit in chairs facing them. The room is silent. The male Scientist clears his throat.

"My name is Carey and I worked to help build the State. I was an aerospace engineer. For years I worked for a company that built shuttles that would travel to other planets. But we lost funding, and government officials approached me about their plan to build an underground superstructure. They knew nuclear war was a real threat."

"They wanted to build it to protect the government." I knew this much.

"Actually"—the woman Scientist looks at Carey—"that's only partly true."

Rhen leans forward. "What?"

"The government couldn't afford the costs of building the State." Carey's voice is quiet. "So they allowed wealthy individuals to purchase a pod, promising they could live in the State in the event of a nuclear war."

John's eyes are wide. "I never knew that."

"We didn't know either." Carey shakes his head. "There were many things we didn't know."

"Go on." I want to hear more. How much of what we were taught were lies?

"We didn't find out about that until much later," Carey says. "When I came on, all I knew was I had a government grant to help construct the superstructure so it could survive a nuclear attack. Once those plans were in place, I helped develop the blueprints for the pods. We used the most state-of-the-art material we could find, knowing it might not be able to be replaced or repaired for many years."

"They have held up well." Rhen nods. "Everything has."

"Everything but the oxygen." The woman doesn't say this with malice. She seems truly saddened about this fact. "Sorry, I am Kristie. Before working for the State, I developed technology to make hyperbaric chambers."

"You were an expert in managing oxygen." Which is why she is so concerned about the oxygen levels in the State. Those were her creations.

"Yes." Kristie sighs. "I was so young when I started there. Barely thirty. I thought I was helping to save humanity. I was sure we could come up with something huge. The Scientists working there were the best in the country, and we were all working toward the same goal. Or so I thought."

"At first, we were." Carey places his hand on Kristie's knee. "But when the War actually happened, things changed."

"Because there was no warning?"

Carey and Kristie exchange a look before Carey continues. "Is that what you were told?"

"Yes." I swallow hard.

"We had equipment that allowed us to monitor the locations of the countries around the world that had nuclear weapons."

"You knew the attack was coming?" I have never seen John angry. His face is red and he stands up, moving away from Carey and Kristie.

"*We* didn't." Kristie stands and takes John's hands in her own. "Please believe me. If we had known, we would have contacted the president immediately."

"Some of the Scientists felt that the current government was not worth saving."

"So they didn't tell them?"

"No." Kristie takes a deep breath. "Nor did they tell those who had invested in the pods."

"But the military had radars," John says. "They knew. The White House knew. Right?"

Carey lowers his head. "We had the most brilliant minds in the country. Rerouting all information through our headquarters was simple."

"They kept that information from the government?" John's voice is louder than I have ever heard it.

"They didn't trust the president." Kristie folds her arms across her chest. "They didn't like him."

"Let me make sure I understand this." Berk leans forward. "You are saying the Scientists knew the attack was coming, and they refused to save anyone?"

"They were part of the attack." Kristie looks at John, her eyes sad. "They moved our weapons into position, forcing the enemy countries to do the same. Then once our weapons were discharged, the other countries responded in kind."

"The Scientists destroyed the whole world." I can hardly believe what I am saying, what I am hearing.

John is sitting now, his head in his hands. He is rocking back and forth. His voice is so muffled I can hardly hear him. "James Turner? Did he know?"

"James?" Carey says. "No, no, James was unaware. Spires, Loudin, and Williams made that choice. James was just as angry as the rest of us were."

John takes a ragged breath. "Good. Good. Thank you."

"But when it was over, we were divided," Kristie continues. "Loudin believed we had the chance to make an evolutionary jump, to create a new, better version of man."

"Without emotions to cloud our judgment and create conflict." Berk shakes his head—we know these reasons.

"Yes." Carey nods. "And in that, they meant well. The world was so dangerous, with so much evil and hate and fear. They were sure that if the government were allowed in, they would simply rebuild another country to mirror the one destroyed."

"But what about the others?" I cannot help thinking of those who paid for the State to be built. They paid for my life with theirs.

Carey shrugs. "Loudin said they were more of the same—greedy, selfish, and concerned with power. He felt we needed to start with just the fifteen of us."

CHAPTER THIRTEEN

ifteen?" I feel like the room is spinning. "What do you mean fifteen? There are ten Scientists. *The* Ten."

"Ten remained," Kristie says. "Five of us could not agree to their plan. We didn't want to create new people. We believed people could be taught to be better. We believed families are important."

"Emotions too." Carey takes Kristie's hand in his.

"But we were outnumbered."

Berk blinks several times. "But how did you escape so soon after the War?"

"We didn't leave immediately," Carey says. "For a while, we were all in survival mode."

"When things settled down, though, Loudin outlined his plan. And he had the others firmly on his side." Kristie bites her lip. "The Geneticists had already begun creating the first generation."

Carey bows his head. "They started with a hundred. But so many had severe mutations, only thirty made it to term."

"It was when we saw those babies that we knew we had to leave." Tears spring from Kristie's eyes. "So much death, so much pain. A 70 percent fail rate. And they were thrilled."

"We all knew a few places aboveground survived." Carey places an arm around Kristie's shoulders. "The bombs were pointed at the major cities across the world, and the effects would radiate far beyond. But there are places—places like this—far enough from any major city that they were not destroyed."

"But how did you escape so soon after the War?" I think of all the precautions we took—forty years after the War had taken place.

"We escaped much like you did." Carey stands and walks to a cabinet. He opens it and pulls out a suit—one exactly like ours but yellowed with age and dusty from disuse. "Three of us snuck old motorcycles down before the War for sentimental value. We rode those here. Somehow we managed to dig up enough gas from the rubble to keep them going."

"The Designer was protecting you," John says.

"Maybe." Carey shrugs. "But whatever—or whoever—it was, we found our way here, to New Hope."

"New Hope?" I like the way that sounds. I like the way it makes me feel.

"Yes," Kristie says. "We helped the people here start over. We teach at the school. We raised our children here."

"We even helped raise our grandchildren." Carey winks.

"We tried to help make a place that will one day be able to combat what the Scientists in the State are creating. Not with war or anger, but with education and hard work."

The room falls silent. There is much to consider. Fifteen Scientists. Loudin murdering whole countries and lying to his own. Seventy percent dead. New Hope.

I feel caught between two worlds. The State is even more terrible than I realized, and I am ashamed of it. But it is also home, all I have ever known. But I was an anomaly there.

Am I any less of an anomaly here?

CHAPTER FOURTEEN

have to get away. I walk out of the large building. Berk calls after me but I keep moving. I cannot think in there . . . I cannot listen to any more. My brain feels as if it is full of the ashy ground we passed as we traveled here.

I do not know where to go. I just walk. I keep my eyes down. I do not want to see these buildings, the pods. I do not want to see the people. And they do not want to see me. No one is out. They are all inside. I hear muffled voices and know they are close but frightened. Let them be frightened. I am frightened too.

I never really thought ahead to what this village might be like, what we would find here. I worried that the people might be mutated. I worried that they might be violent. I worried that they wouldn't exist. But never, in all my worrying and thinking, did I ever consider this. The Ten were Fifteen? And Dr. Loudin made the choice to attack countries around the world—some neutral—because he wanted to create a better world than the old one?

"Thalli," John calls out. He is winded. I cannot believe he followed me. He needs to rest.

"Please, John." I stop, but only because I want him to do the same. "I can't go back there right now."

"Neither can I." John takes a deep breath.

I suddenly realize that this information is far more personal, far more painful, to him than it is to me. His son is one of the Ten. Even if Dr. Turner wasn't privy to Dr. Loudin's plans when he made them, Dr. Turner chose to abide by them once they were made. He was the head Geneticist. "Where are you going?"

I link an arm through John's. "I don't know."

"May I come?"

I don't answer. I just begin walking. He cannot go far, so I ask the Designer to help us find a place fast. I feel a little sick as I make the request. I have been so angry with him lately. So full of doubts. So focused on myself. What right have I to make any request?

"There." John points to a strange-looking structure. Two large triangles made from cut trees support a post that looks weathered. From that post hang two objects. "Swings."

"What?" I watch as John moves quicker.

"Swings." John sits on one of the objects. It moves with him. He lifts his feet and smiles broadly. "We used to push our children on these for hours. I built them a huge swing set in our backyard. Two swings, a slide, a fort, a climbing wall. It took me months. But the kids loved it. I was fixing it up before I came out to visit James. We were planning on our grandkids using it."

John never got to see his grandchildren. He came out to visit Dr. Turner just before the Nuclear War hit, before his daughter had her first child. He spent the last forty years locked up in the State, a virtual prisoner, allowed only to speak to those scheduled for annihilation. He was seen as a danger to the citizens because of his faith.

"Sit." John points to the object beside him. "It's fun."

I lower myself onto the narrow rectangular seat. The ropes holding it move and I almost fall. I hold on to them with both hands to make them stop moving and I sit. I move slowly at first—back and forth.

"Walk backward and then pick up your feet."

I can imagine John saying this to his children. There is such joy in his eyes. I cannot refuse, despite my fear at the instability of this swing. I do as he says, holding on to the ropes with all my strength. My heart feels as if it has dropped into my stomach. But the sensation is exciting. Fun.

John laughs as I swing higher, following his instructions to "pump" my legs. I feel as if I could touch the sky with my feet. I lean back and close my eyes. The sensation is unlike anything I have ever experienced.

"You have missed out on so much." John's voice is sad. I am sure he is thinking about the world before the War.

"Why would Dr. Loudin do that?" I look at John, slowing my swing with my feet. "Was the world so terrible that it needed to be destroyed?"

"Have I ever told you about Noah?"

"I don't think so." Did John hear my question? I want to ask again but he begins speaking.

"In the Designer's book, there is the story of a man named Noah." John stands and stretches his arms over his head. "The world had become evil. People were ignoring the Designer, angering him. So he decided to destroy it. All of it. With a world-wide flood. Because Noah was a righteous man, the Designer spared him and his family."

"That's terrible."

"It sounds terrible, yes," John says. "But the Designer is the Designer. Everything he does is good. It is just."

"You think Dr. Loudin was acting like the Designer?"

"I think Dr. Loudin believed he could be like the Designer." John shakes his head. "James believed the same thing. That there is no Designer. That man is the highest power. They believed they knew what was best for the world. The Scientists were sure they knew how to re-create the world into a better place. Without emotion and religion and conflict."

"But they did, didn't they? With the exception of anomalies like me?"

John walks to me and places his soft hands on my face. "You are not an anomaly. You are fearfully and wonderfully made. And no, the Scientists did not create a better place. A world without the Designer is not better. It is a world without hope, without true joy, without love."

I know John is right, but I still struggle with it. Feeling so much seems wrong. Doubting the Scientists seems wrong. It goes against all I have been taught.

I glance at John and notice he has closed his eyes, his lips moving, eyebrows furrowed. John prays at all times. I wait as he finishes. He opens his eyes and lets out a deep sigh. "It is James. The Designer is impressing upon me to pray for him. God is not through with my son."

I want to ask how he knows that, what he means, but John is looking at something else, something beyond me. I turn to see Berk limping toward us. "I think I'd better head back. I'll see you later."

I am suddenly sick to my stomach. I don't know what to say to Berk. I am afraid of what he will say. Afraid to hear he has developed feelings for Rhen. Truthfully, he and Rhen are better suited for each other than he and I. She is logical, careful. And now she seems to be developing abnormal feelings. But not completely abnormal, like mine. She doesn't lose control and cry or question or get angry. She is just softer and kinder. Berk deserves someone like her. She is better than me in every way.

John pauses to whisper something in Berk's ear. Berk nods but he doesn't smile. I cannot identify the look in his eyes, but I do not like it. It makes me uncomfortable. Nervous. He keeps walking toward me. I didn't even notice when I stood and turned around. I cannot think clearly where Berk is concerned.

"Thalli." He is standing in front of me, his gaze locked on mine. "It is time to talk."

CHAPTER FIFTEEN

do not like the way he said that. His eyes weren't soft. His voice wasn't gentle. He seemed more like "Dr. Berk" than the Berk I have come to know.

"Can we walk a little?" His voice is higher pitched than normal. It is not the smooth melody of a trombone, but the pinched tone of a French horn. He is still limping, his leg not completely healed from the attack.

"Have you seen the healer yet?"

"Not yet." He looks ahead, the silence between us almost tangible. He seems to know where we are going. His legs are longer than mine, so even with his injury, I struggle to keep up.

Now as I walk, I look everywhere. I need my mind to be occupied with something else—anything else.

I walk past a faded blue pod with pieces of cut trees on parts of the top. The window fabric is pulled back, and I see a living area with a variety of furniture. I stop to look closer. I cannot help myself. The fabrics remind me of John's room: colorful, patterned, aged. Learning pads appear to be everywhere, but that cannot be. There is no technology here. No electricity. These pads are still. Just pictures. But pictures of what I assume are families. I am still uncomfortable with that thought. John told me about families, about marriage and children, but that is so different from the world of my experience.

Berk has not stopped, and when I look for him, I see he is far ahead. I jog to keep up with him. He doesn't look back at me. I look beyond him and see a hill. It is similar to the hill we walked over to arrive here, but this one has blue flowers all over it and the grass is thicker.

Berk is at the top of the hill. He finally looks back and watches me as I climb to meet him.

"Where are we?" I am breathing heavily. The hill is steeper than I expected.

"Look." Berk motions below. "A lake."

I see water. A lot of water. "A lake." It is beautiful. The sun reflects off the ripples created by the wind. Leaves drift onto the surface and float along. Birds are flying overhead and cows are drinking at its banks. I have never seen anything like it. It is so much bigger than the pond John swam in when we first arrived.

"Sit."

I sink into the grass, enjoying the feel of it between my fingers.

"We haven't spoken much lately." Berk is still looking at the lake.

"You have been busy." I shrug. "And hurt."

"I am recovering well." Berk states the obvious. Will our entire conversation be this uncomfortable?

We are silent. Again. I know what he wants to say. And I know why he cannot bring himself to say it. "Berk, it's all right. You and Rhen. I understand." I don't know how I got those words out without crying, but I did.

"What?"

"I've seen you." I turn and look at him. His green eyes are wide and I cannot look away. "You have feelings for her. And that's all right. I understand."

"I have feelings for Rhen?" Berk stands there, his jaw flexing. "And you *understand*?"

I stand and brush the grass from my fingers. Why is he angry? He should be relieved, not angry.

"Thalli." Berk takes a step closer to me, places his hands on the sides of my face. I feel the heat from his touch, thawing what I thought was frozen. "How can you think that?"

I can't think when Berk is touching me. I pull away, examine the grass. "You were with her all the time."

"You almost died, Thalli." Berk waves his arms. "Your body was still processing the toxins from the annihilation chamber. Your emotions were all over the place. We were trying to spare you needless stress."

"You were trying to spare me?" I am not sure what in his last statement didn't offend me. I feel my heart freezing again. "You almost died too, Berk. You were barely able to walk."

"But my mind wasn't compromised."

"And mine was?" If he wants to see emotions out of control, he will see it. "Was it compromised when I saved your life? When I carried the chamber and helped John? Is that what you and Rhen were talking about? Poor, deluded Thalli. She spent too long in the annihilation chamber. Let's ignore her so she doesn't get upset and do something to endanger us all."

Berk opens his mouth and closes it. His self-control, apparently, is also superior to mine.

"Say it, Berk." I push his shoulders with my hands. "Go ahead."

Berk takes a step back and shakes his head. He is leaving. I want to stop him. I want to apologize, to grab him and hold him and beg him to choose me over Rhen. But I do not. I cannot. I stand in place, watching Berk walk away, wishing he had left me in the State.

CHAPTER SIXTEEN

Hey, new girl." A boy about my age, with dark hair and eyes, olive complexion, tall, and very muscular, runs up to me, his white smile wide.

I have been in New Hope for three days. Carey and Kristie have given us rooms in what they call their home—part of the large structure we first saw when we arrived. Berk and John are on the opposite end as Rhen and me. They have been spending their days at the healer's. John seems to be moving better, so I suppose it is working.

I have not spoken to Berk, have only seen him in passing. I have spent my days reading. I read the book by Dickens, a story of a boy who loves a girl who treats him terribly and doesn't love the girl who truly loves him. I am not sure if I feel more like the boy in the story, the terrible girl, or the good one.

I decided to take a walk outside, avoiding the path to the lake where Berk and I fought. But within minutes of starting, this boy approached, smiling as if he knows me.

"Dallas." He holds out his hand.

"Excuse me?"

"The name's Dallas." He takes my hand in his and moves it up and down before releasing it. "I'm Carey and Kristie's grandson."

The idea of a grandson is so strange. I have to think for a moment what that is. "I am Thalli."

"Thalli, huh?" Dallas has trouble saying my name properly. As if his name is easy to pronounce. "I met Rhen. She is something."

"Something what?"

"I mean something." Dallas spreads his hands wide. "As in . . . really cool."

"Cool?" I have found the atmosphere here to be quite warm, with a wetness to the air that makes my skin damp and my thick brown hair curl more than usual, causing it to lie heavier down my back.

Dallas shakes his head. "It's like we speak a different language."

"I would like to learn more about yours." I cannot help liking this friendly young man. He seems so comfortable with himself. "We hope to make our home here."

"I'm glad to hear that." Dallas smiles and starts walking. I fall into step beside him. "You and Rhen are just about the best-looking girls I've ever seen. I know you have a thing for Berg—"

"His name is Berk, and I don't . . ."

"The dude is hot. I get it. If I were a chick, I'd be into him too."

I have no idea what Dallas is talking about, but neither his mouth nor his legs slow down, so I remain quiet and let him continue.

"But Rhen—she doesn't have a boyfriend, does she? I mean, it's just the four of you, right? No one else?"

"Correct."

"So if you're with Berk, and the old guy is just old, then Rhen is available?"

"Available?"

"No boyfriend?"

"Boyfriend?" I'm familiar with the words, but they seem to carry more of a meaning than what I know.

Dallas groans. "Someone she likes, that she's dating? Like you and Berk?"

I want to tell him Berk and I are not what he thinks we are, but I cannot get those words out.

"Forget it." Dallas slows down. "That was rude of me—introduce myself and try to get info from you about your best friend. Mom would kill me."

"She would kill you?" I thought this village was peaceable.

Dallas laughs—a loud, genuine sound that makes me smile. "It's a saying. My mom wouldn't actually kill me. But she has tried to teach me to be polite to people. *Tried* being the key word there."

I'm still not entirely sure I understand Dallas, but I keep smiling anyway.

"Want to see our farm?" Dallas speeds up again.

I recall Rhen telling me she has been spending time on a farm. She mentioned horses and trees. But she has not mentioned

Dallas. Of course, we have not spoken much. I have been busy reading. I don't care if it is a primitive form of entertainment. I find reading about others' problems to be quite soothing. And it keeps me from having to hear from Rhen what I do not wish to hear.

I follow Dallas past a grouping of trees. Orange trees. The oranges aren't perfect, like the ones grown in the greenhouses in the State, but there are many of them. Some are on the ground, turning brown. I stop to examine one and see tiny insects crawling around the rind, dirt and grass around the trunk. A light wind lifts my hair, bringing with it the scent of oranges. So different but so beautiful.

"You coming?" Dallas is far ahead of me, and I race to catch up with him.

In the distance, a large building looms. As we get closer, the smell of oranges is replaced by a smell far less pleasant. A young girl with hair and eyes as dark as the minor keys on a piano runs out of the building and leaps into Dallas's arms.

"D!" She looks at me and grins—revealing a hole where her two front teeth should be. "Is this the girl you like?"

Dallas turns red and lowers the girl to the ground. "That's Nicole—my sister. Nicole, this is Thalli."

"You didn't answer my question."

Dallas turns to look at a pod on the other side of the large building. Rhen steps out of it and waves at us.

Nicole laughs. "*That's* the girl you like."

I am not sure how to respond to this conversation, so I walk ahead to greet Rhen.

"Peter was about to take me to the horses." Rhen sounds so excited. I have never seen her like this. "Come with us."

I look behind her to see a blond young man walk out of the house. He appears to be older than I am, shorter than Dallas, but just as muscular. His face seems much sadder than Dallas's, though.

"If you want a tour of the stables, I'm your guy." Dallas takes Rhen's arm and moves with her toward the building. I follow. "Peter is new here. He doesn't know much about the place. We just let him bunk with us because we're such good people."

Rhen and I look at one another. "He's new here?"

Dallas shrugs. "Escaped from Athens a few weeks ago."

Peter turns around and starts walking. "I need to run into town for a couple things, all right?"

"Doesn't like to talk about it," Dallas whispers as he moves Rhen toward the building again. "Good guy, hard worker. We'll get him back on his feet again. Grams says he just needs some time and space to sort everything out."

"Is Athens so terrible?"

"They're just mean." Dallas stops at a huge double door that is taller than I have ever seen. "They think they can just take what they want because they are stronger and have more technology than us. But we've got the food. So they attack us and steal from us to try to get what they need."

"That is horrible." These are the primitive people our history lessons warned us about.

"That's probably not even the worst." Dallas pulls at the door and it makes loud noises as it opens. "They keep to themselves. Peter talks to my grandparents, but he won't say a word to the rest of us about why he left."

Dallas guides us inside, where half a dozen horses congregate. They are beautiful creatures. A little frightening but beautiful. Dallas walks right up to the one closest to us and strokes its neck. "This one is Sugar. She's my favorite. I've taken care of her since she was a baby."

Dallas pulls an apple from a bag hanging on a wall, and I watch, fascinated, as the horse eats the whole thing in three bites. He goes on to show us all the horses, tells us their names, and gives them all an apple. Actually, he is telling Rhen. I just happen to be in the building too. Dallas is obviously as intrigued by my beautiful friend as Berk is. Dallas's attention, though, gives me a feeling that is exactly the opposite of what I feel when she is near Berk.

Rhen and I walk back to the village. Dallas insists on walking with us. With Rhen. I want to tell him to give up. Rhen belongs with Berk now. But Dallas is so eager. And perhaps I am hoping he will draw her attentions away from Berk.

I look around, though, and feel the wind, smell the scents of animals and fruits and so much more. Do I want Berk as much as I thought? Did I love him because he was the only one like me in the State? Someone with feelings and questions? Or is there more? Do I love him the way John loved Amy?

I think of Dallas. I do not feel anything for him, but I do appreciate that he is so open with his emotions. So honest. I wish Berk were more like that. I do not know what he is thinking most of the time. I do not like that he keeps secrets from me. I find that the more I am here, the more I like it. I could belong here. I am different because of the way I speak, but not because of who I am. Emotions are natural here. Freedom is given here. And best of all, here in New Hope, I am not an anomaly.

CHAPTER SEVENTEEN

We have been here for two weeks, and no Monitors have come. The Scientists likely assume we perished in our escape. They would not have wasted manpower trying to discover our bodies. I feel safe for the first time in my life. My friends are safe—this thought brings an even greater peace.

Berk and I have still barely spoken. He is focused on learning the way of life here, of talking with the Scientists, of being useful. When we do speak it is strained, uncomfortable. I do not know what to say to him. I can sense he feels the same. The easy communication that existed between us is gone. Able to survive only in the pressurized world of the State? I try not to think about that. I focus instead on the freedom I have, the peace.

I have joined Rhen and am learning to work in the orchards, to care for horses. Little Nicole has become my companion in all things agrarian. She is delightful—so open, so happy. I ask questions about her life, trying to better understand the concept of parents, siblings, learning about aunts, uncles, cousins. She teaches me more about her language. I now know the different definitions of *cool* and *hot*. I know the names of the winds that blow past and the types of weather to expect here. I have seen rain, felt breezes, but have yet to experience snow, tornadoes, and heat waves.

Sometimes I walk out in the groves, just enjoying the feel of the sun on my skin. It is a feeling unlike anything I have ever known. I understand John better as well—what he has missed all the years he was below. He is so happy in New Hope. We all are. Mostly.

I am learning to release Berk's hold on my heart. It still hurts, like a wound that pulls at my flesh. But it will heal. I know it will. And I will be stronger for it.

"Excuse me." Peter bumps into me, his arms laden with a basket full of oranges.

"Can I help you?" I open the barn door and follow him in. Peter is the exact opposite of Dallas—he barely speaks and rarely smiles. He is from Athens, but that is all I know. He is new here, though, like me. I want to know what New Hope feels like to him. I want to know what Athens is like. I have so many questions I'd like to ask Peter. If I could just make him talk.

"Sure." Peter sets the basket down and begins placing the

oranges in three different bins. One bin will go to the house and two to the store.

"How long have you been here?"

Peter drops an armful of oranges into the house bin and sighs. "Not long."

"Do you miss Athens?"

The look Peter gives me makes all other questions disintegrate. It's anger mixed with something else, something I can't define. "No."

I remember now that Dallas said Peter doesn't like to talk about Athens. As much as I want to ask him more, I need to remain silent. We finish the bins in half an hour, the only sounds in the barn coming from the animals nearby.

"I'm going to shower, then I'll take the oranges up to the store." Peter walks toward the house. Dallas told me Peter shares a room with him. His parents volunteered to give Peter a home when he arrived in exchange for his help around the farm. "Thanks for your help."

I begin walking back to my home... such a strange thought. My home. Not my pod or cube or chamber. Home. It sounds so warm, so peaceful.

I am halfway there when the ground shakes suddenly. I cover my ears but the noise still reaches my eardrums, threatens to pierce them. Is it a tornado? Nicole said they are loud when they are close. But she also said the sky is dark when they come and usually rainy. It is bright and clear above. Yet the noise persists.

Then it is over. As quickly as it started. I don't know what happened. I feel dazed. I look around. Smoke pours from the village. What is it from? It was not there just minutes before. The smell is horrible. People are screaming.

I run out of the grove and I see Dallas and Nicole's house on fire. Peter just walked in there minutes before. A huge hole looks like it has been carved out of the center. In the distance, a group of people are galloping on horses toward the village. They hold large sticks with fire on the ends.

I run as fast as I can toward the house. What if Nicole and her family were in there along with Peter? I see others running from the village toward the house. I see Rhen's blond hair. Breathing deeply, I slow. Rhen will reach them. She will help.

I stop to gulp in lungsful of oxygen before running again. When I get there, Rhen is on her knees beside an unconscious Peter. I place a hand over my mouth, look at Rhen for information about his condition.

"His pulse is steady." Rhen's voice is calm in the midst of all the chaos. "But we need to get him away from here."

Two men gather Peter in their arms and carry him toward a pod farther off. Kristie is at the edge of the crowd, tears in her eyes as she looks at the house.

"What happened? Who did this?" I ask quietly.

Kristie looks at me, anger in her eyes. "The Athenians."

I hear commotion in the village. People yelling, screaming for food. "Is that them?"

"Yes."

"What do we do?"

"Stay here for now." Kristie pulls me into the barn. "Carey will give them what they ask for."

"Why?"

"Because if we don't, they will kill us."

I think of Peter lying unconscious outside the burning house. "Why would they do that?"

"They have less fertile soil than we do." Kristie lowers herself onto the ground. I join her. "And they use most of it to grow the ingredients for the medicines they are creating. They struggle to grow crops and keep animals alive. So they come here and take our food and our animals."

"But that is barbaric." I want to go outside and shout at these people for what they are doing. Stealing food? Killing people?

"It is. But it is all they know. We have tried to reason with them, to work with them, but they refuse to listen."

I cannot comprehend this. It is like a lesson from my learning pad about the ancient civilizations, but this isn't a lesson. It is actually happening. And it is horrible.

"It has gotten worse since Peter escaped and ran here."

"Why did he escape?"

"They wanted him to finish what his grandparents started."

"His grandparents?"

"I told you five of us escaped: Carey and me, Emile, Janet, and Victor. We all stayed here for a while. Until Victor got sick. Cancer." Kristie closes her eyes. "He was in so much pain. Emile had been a developer of pharmaceuticals, so he tried to see what he could find to duplicate medicines to help Victor. But there wasn't enough time. Victor died a terrible death. Carey and I were upset."

"I can imagine."

"But Emile and Janet." Kristie takes a deep breath. "They were angry. So angry. They refused to stay here. The other surviving town . . ."

"Athens?"

"Yes." Kristie picks up a piece of hay and rolls it with her fingers. "They sent people over, wanting our help. But they wanted to rebuild everything that was destroyed, with themselves as leaders—rulers. They wanted to rule with power, to use warfare to force people into submission. We refused to help them. We wanted to live peaceful lives, focusing on families and education. We didn't see the benefit of trying to regain the technological advances from before the War. And we certainly did not want to see any more war. Never again. But after Victor died, Emile and Janet changed their minds. They didn't want war, but neither did they want anyone to experience what Victor experienced. They were sure they could convince the Athenians to focus on medicine and not warfare."

"Obviously that didn't work."

Kristie sighs. "They never spoke to us after that. We tried to visit, but the Athenians refused to even let us in their town. It is surrounded by a large wall and guarded at all times."

"But Peter escaped."

"It was difficult. But he had no choice. His grandparents developed pharmaceuticals. Strong ones. They died without completing the work. He refused to continue it."

I have so many more questions—each new piece of information makes me hungry to learn so much more. But pain is heavy in Kristie's eyes, and I should remain silent for now. Save my questions. We sit in silence until the sounds of the Athenians fade into the distance.

"We must return to our house." Kristie stands and wipes dirt from her pants. "There will be chaos in the village."

CHAPTER EIGHTEEN

Dozens of people are crowded in Kristie and Carey's home. The smell of smoke lingers on them, and I cough to expel it from my lungs.

"They're going too far now." A man with a long beard points his finger at Kristie.

"Peter could have died," another man says. "They targeted him specifically. How did they even know which house was his?"

"They're watching us, I tell you." The first man turns to the crowd. "They've got all that equipment. They can do anything. And we just sit back and let them."

Several people begin talking at once. Some say they need to fight the Athenians; others say they'd be killed if they tried. The man with the beard shouts that they need to build a wall, but a woman argues the Athenians will just shoot their cannons over it or burn it down.

"So let's burn theirs down," the bearded man says. "Fight fire with fire."

More shouting. My ears are still ringing from the blast, and this makes them ache even more.

Kristie stands on a chair and raises her arms. "Enough." Her voice is not loud, but she speaks with authority, and surprisingly, the people stop shouting. "I agree that something must be done. But we will not respond in kind. We have agreed to avoid war. Our town is built upon a foundation of peace, and we will maintain that position."

"And let those Athenians drive us out?" the bearded man shouts. "The time for peace is over. We didn't start this, but we can finish it."

Everyone has an opinion on this, and they all seem to be sharing it at the same time. I can't hear any one person, just a cacophony of angry voices, like a hundred piano keys being banged at the same time.

Kristie is trying to restore order, but no one listens. Then a young woman walks in, and every person stops talking. She is about the same age as me, with reddish-brown hair, fair skin, and big brown eyes that look frightened. Her hands are shaking. Most of the crowd looks at her with anger.

Only Kristie takes a step toward her. "Who are you?"

"Diana." Her voice is so quiet, I can barely hear the next words. "I am Peter's sister."

A collective gasp sounds, and Kristie puts an arm around Diana.

"Where is my brother?" Diana looks into Kristie's eyes. "Is he all right?"

"I'll take you to him." Kristie turns to face the crowd. "The rest of you go home now. We'll discuss this later."

Murmurs abound but no one speaks as Kristie leads Diana away.

"Thalli." Kristie looks at me. "Come with us. I don't want to leave you here right now, not with the people as angry as they are."

I gladly obey. We walk back outside. The fire has been put out, but the smoke still lingers and the ash that drifts down reminds me of the ground outside the State.

"How did you get here?" Kristie keeps her arm around Diana's frail shoulders.

"I hid in the back of the car."

"The car?" I didn't think those existed anymore.

Kristie looks at me. "The Athenians pull a car with horses and they fill it up with food from New Hope."

"Oh." I recall seeing the other vehicle being pulled when we arrived. Transportation here is so different.

"I heard them planning to attack Peter. They discovered his location . . . they want to kill him." Diana begins to cry. "I had to stop them. But I couldn't do anything."

Kristie doesn't say anything. She allows Diana to cry and then waits for her to speak again. "It happened so fast. They didn't even wait until we were close. I thought we had several more minutes left. The car didn't even stop. I didn't know."

"Of course you didn't." Kristie pulls the young woman into

a hug. "Peter is in the clinic now, but I believe he is all right. He wasn't hit. He was trapped in the house for a few minutes, but some of our people were able to get him out."

I cannot believe people would actually try to kill another human being. But then I am reminded that right before my escape from the State, I was in an annihilation room. My death would have been more humane than a fire. The gas would have put me to sleep and then my organs would have shut down while I was unconscious. But murder is murder. Are these Athenians any more or less barbaric because they use fire rather than gas?

"In here." Kristie points to a pod that is smaller than her own quarters but larger than the ones they call "houses." The clinic must be the equivalent of our medical facilities. The room has a strange mixture of smells. The first is smoke, although I am becoming accustomed to that now. The second stings my nose and brings tears to my eyes.

We walk through the first room, one with several chairs and a window in one wall, to a second room. This one is very small and has an oddly shaped sleeping platform. Peter is lying on it. His eyes are open but they are red. His face is smudged with black.

"Peter."

"Diana." Peter's voice is barely audible. As soon as he says his sister's name, he begins coughing. I turn away as he spits into a bowl on a table beside him. Rhen comes in with a container filled with water and hands it to Peter.

"Will he be all right?"

A man enters behind Rhen and looks from Diana to Peter. "He should be fine, but he will need to rest for several days."

"Does he need to be on oxygen?" Kristie asks. "There should be some in the back."

"No, he will recover without it." The man waves Kristie off with his hands. "We need to save that."

"But he can't even talk." Diana looks at the man.

"He just needs time." The man puts a hand on Diana's arm. "I have seen this before. When Dallas fell asleep at the bonfire. Remember, Kristie?"

She nods. "I certainly do remember. We were all out looking for him—Dallas couldn't have been more than five or six at the time. We were so frightened. And there he was, sound asleep beside the ashes. I was sure he would suffer permanent damage."

"I'm not so sure he didn't." The man laughs.

"Hey, I heard that." Dallas enters the room, his smile undeterred by the circumstances. "And it wasn't my fault you fed me so full that I fell asleep. And who left me there, huh? My own grandparents."

Kristie runs her hands through Dallas's dark hair.

"You gonna be okay, Peter?"

Peter nods at Dallas. He is probably too frightened of coughing to speak again.

"Good, 'cause I'm stuck doing all your chores while you're sick." Dallas rolls his eyes. "I don't know how you stand cleaning up after the horses. Must be 'cause they stink as bad as you do."

"Dallas." Kristie pulls her grandson away from Peter. "This is Diana. Peter's sister."

"Sorry to meet under these circumstances." Dallas holds a hand out to Diana. "But we're glad to have you both here. And Peter can tell you, we take good care of refugees. Right, Peter?"

He coughs in response.

"If you're looking for a job, we've got an opening for a stable girl."

Peter waves his hand, a weak smile covering his face. "Please."

"Aw, look, Peter's begging to keep that job." Dallas laughs. "All right, buddy. I won't give it away."

Peter points a finger toward the door.

"I know you wanna get back to work, but you have to rest." Dallas backs up as Peter picks up a cup and tries to throw it at his friend.

"Your brother doesn't have very good manners, does he?" Dallas winks at Diana. He closes the door before Peter tosses a medicine bottle at him.

Kristie smiles, then squeezes Diana's arm. "I need to see how the rest of the town is doing. Is it all right if I leave you here for now?"

"Yes, of course." Diana's gaze doesn't leave her brother. I don't even think she noticed Dallas was here. "Thank you."

We walk out the door and I see that night is beginning to fall. With it comes the realization that I am exhausted. Beyond exhausted. So much has happened. I can hardly even comprehend all of it. I need to think through everything, to sort it all out. But all I can think about is sleep.

Kristie takes me back to my room, and I sink into the bed without even removing my clothing. I pull off my shoes, relax into the softness, and sleep.

CHAPTER NINETEEN

"W e must act!" An angry voice wakes me up.

"Gerald, please." Carey's voice is softer. I can only hear a few words.

"Guests . . . peace . . . dangerous."

"If we let this go, they will just get worse." I recognize the voice now—the bearded man. "Peace only works if both sides agree. They want war, Carey, and they'll have it whether we agree or not."

I run a hand through my tangled hair and slip into my shoes. I don't know if our presence exacerbated these problems or not, but as we're part of this community, their problems are ours. I do not want to be shielded from them.

"Thalli." Kristie walks to me. Carey is standing inches away from the bearded man's— Gerald's—face. He is speaking quietly. Kristie tries to pull me into another room, but I ease her hand away and walk over to the men.

"Please tell me what is going on."

"Me too." Berk walks into the room. His light brown hair is messy. He doesn't look at me.

"What's going on," Gerald begins, "is that these folks have gone from simple threats to out-and-out warfare. A cannon. That's what they shot into that house yesterday. A burning cannon. Peter could have been killed. Dallas's parents could have been killed. If we don't retaliate, they'll just do it again. What if it's you next time? Or Dallas? Or little Nicole?"

"I understand your concern." Carey looks to Kristie, an unspoken message passing between them. "But we need to think logically about this. We can't afford to respond emotionally. Nothing good will come of that."

Gerald's face gets so red, he looks as if he'll explode. He stomps out the door and slams it.

"I'm sorry." Carey falls into the chair. Kristie sits on the couch and I join her.

Still refusing to meet my gaze, Berk takes a seat beside me. "What can we do?"

"We have a town meeting planned for later this morning." Carey runs a hand through his red, thinning hair. "We'll discuss it all then."

"How many people agree with Gerald?" Will this meeting be similar to the shouting crowd who came here yesterday?

"I'm not exactly sure," Carey says. "He is an agitator, and you can be sure he has visited everyone in town, giving them his opinion. He has been working for years to get an army together. I believe he is close to achieving that."

"You should eat and bathe and relax a little before all of this." Kristie stands, cutting off the conversation.

I want to know more, but I follow Kristie's lead. I go to my closet to find clean clothes. These clothes are not like ours, but I like all the colors. I choose a pink shirt and a blue pair of pants. Rhen still prefers plain colors.

I smile to myself as I realize I feel less and less a part of the State. That Thalli from the State is disappearing, being made into Thalli from New Hope. But my smile fades. This new Thalli is one without Berk. The longer we avoid speaking to one another, the harder it will be to start again. And I don't think I can be the first to speak. Not when he accused me of being compromised, when he justified his time alone with Rhen because I was "recovering" from the annihilation chamber.

I shake my head. I may have lost Berk, but I have new friends—Nicole and Dallas, Kristie and Carey. That is enough.

Perhaps if I say that to myself enough, I will eventually believe it.

CHAPTER TWENTY

The girl can't stay!" Gerald is shouting. Again. Does that man know how to communicate in any other way? "Peter came over and they started burning up our houses. Now his sister is here. Who knows what they'll plan when they find out she escaped too. No way. Uh-uh. She's got to go."

"We can't send Diana back," Carey argues. "She escaped. If we did that, can you imagine what they would do to her?"

"Look, you can't have peace *and* these kids." Gerald's Adam's apple bobs with each word. "Make up your mind. Keep 'em and we need to start defending ourselves. Because the Athenians *will* attack."

"And what about those four?" A friend of Gerald's, if his attitude is any indication, points at Berk, John, Rhen, and me. "How do we know they really escaped from the State? That they aren't just spies from Athens?"

The crowd erupts in shouts, and it's several minutes before Carey quiets them down. "That is enough. All of these kids have gone through far too much for us to treat them with anything but hospitality."

A few people shout, "Hear, hear." My heart warms at their support.

"We do need a strategy to deal with the Athenians, though." Carey leans his head toward Gerald. "They are escalating. This time, they cleaned out the storehouse and took half a dozen cows."

Rumbles begin low throughout the group. Many knew this information already, but it was obvious some were hearing it for the first time.

"I still say we need to build a wall."

"And I still say they'll just burn it."

"Why can't we try to negotiate peace?"

"Last time we tried that, they sent old Jeff back with a broken leg."

Carey silences the crowd once more. "One thing we know: They want us to continue our way of life. Our food supplies them as well. They will not destroy us."

"So we just keep giving them our stuff?" Gerald says. "Because we're scared of 'em? What's gonna stop them from taking more and more? Leaving us nothing?"

"Gerald makes a point."

More shouting and grumbling and arguing ensues.

"What if I go?" I can't even believe I said it. But the words are out. And the people are quiet. "I can gather information about their plans and report it back to you."

"Thalli, no." Berk is beside me, his eyes wide. Now he speaks to me? To tell me no?

"I am new. I am neutral. They will accept me because I am from the State." The more I talk, the surer I am that this is the solution. One that will help New Hope, keep my friends safe, and give Berk time to spend with Rhen without my having to see them together.

"They're dangerous, Thalli." Berk grabs my arm. "You saw what they did."

"Yes, and I agree they may do that again." I pull away. "Or worse. Something has to be done. And no one here can do it. I can."

"Then I should go," Berk says.

"You are still limping." I stare at his leg. He could never walk all the way to Athens. "It has to be me."

"And what if *you* are a spy from Athens?" Gerald steps closer to me. His breath smells like corn. "We just let you go back, tell them what you saw here, and give them the full lay-out of our land?"

"She is not a spy, Gerald." Carey's voice is raised, though still not to the same level as Gerald's. "You're the one who saw them come—from the north, not the west. You saw their equipment. It's not from Athens."

"How would we know that?" Gerald dismisses Carey with his hands. "We don't know what they have in Athens. We've never been there. And who's to say they didn't just come around to the north to throw us off?"

"They've been here two weeks." Dallas steps into the center of the room. "Any of us who have spent any time with them knows they aren't spies. Am I right?"

Several people cheer, and my eyes burn with tears.

"My friends from the State are all here," I shout. "They are the guarantee that I'm not a spy."

The room is quiet again. Even Gerald seems to be considering this.

"All right. You go," Gerald says. "But if it doesn't work, we go in my way. With weapons and an army. We fight for our land."

"Give me two weeks," I say. "That should be enough time to gather information and return."

"One week." Gerald points his finger in my face.

"Then what?" Carey folds his arms.

"Then *I* go in."

"A week isn't enough." I look from Gerald to Carey. "I've been *here* two weeks and there is still so much I don't know."

Carey nods. "But you haven't been focused on learning everything about us. You've just been living."

"You're agreeing with Gerald?" I take in a quick breath.

"'Bout time."

"I am trying to find a compromise." Carey raises his eyebrows at me. "Gerald and I have been friends for a long time. He and his family were kind to us when Kristie and I first got here. He has been part of New Hope since before the War."

"Born and raised right here." Gerald is softening as Carey speaks.

"I know you want what is best for this village, Gerald."

"'Course I do."

"Then let's do all we can to avoid any more bloodshed."

Carey places a hand on Gerald's shoulder. "Give the girl ten days?"

Gerald sucks his teeth, looks from me to Carey and back again. "Fine. But one day you're gonna see that talkin' isn't enough. We've got to fight back. And we're ready. You hear me?"

Voices that have been silent speak out—both in opposition and in support. The noise is so loud, my ears hurt. I look around. There are enough with Gerald to do this, men and women who would die for New Hope. The weight of that reality settles into my heart.

I must go. I must succeed.

Within minutes the crowd is gone. Carey and Kristie tell me all they know about Athens—which isn't much. They have technology, but no one is sure how much or what kind. They prefer power to peace. Something I already surmised on my own. The Scientists who moved there were experts in pharmacology and anatomy. The current king of Athens is ruthless.

"What do I need to find out?" I ask.

Kristie folds her hands in her lap. "We want peace. We want to know what we can do to make that happen. Our two cities should not be at war. We should be working together."

I think of the burning house, of Peter's coughs, and the fear in Diana's eyes. "And if they want nothing to do with peace?"

Carey stands. "Then we need to discover how to defeat them."

CHAPTER TWENTY-ONE

eter is still recovering, but he and Diana are the only two with firsthand knowledge of Athens, and I need to know what they know. Kristie assures me that after a night of good sleep, breathing clean air and being fully hydrated, Peter will be able to hold a conversation. Diana has not left her brother's side, so I find them both in the medical facility. I open the door and hear Dallas talking to Peter.

"Your eyes look like raw meatballs." Dallas's face contorts. "Seriously, you'll never get a girlfriend looking like that."

A pained expression passes over Peter's face. Whether it's from Dallas's assessment of his eyes or his relationship status, I am not sure.

"Thalli." Diana looks up and smiles, though the smile does not reach her eyes. "Kristie told us of your plan."

"Dallas, get out of here." Peter's voice sounds rough, but he speaks without coughing.

"Aw, you know I was just kidding." Dallas backs away. "I didn't really mean you couldn't get a girlfriend because of your eyes."

"Thanks, but I need to talk—"

"It's your ugly face that's gonna keep the girls away." Dallas races out of the room as Peter lobs a container of food at his retreating form.

"I am sorry." Peter pushes himself into a sitting position. The movement seems to be painful for him, but Diana is at his side helping him, giving him water to drink.

I watch her kindness and am filled with a mixture of sadness and anger. I would have liked to have had a sister or brother. Although in many ways I did. My podmates were like siblings. We grew up together, played together, cared for each other. My eyes burn as I think of them. All but Rhen are dead now, "eliminated" because they consumed too much of the State's oxygen. The memory of walking into Pod C, empty of everyone and everything, makes my heart ache.

John tells me I must forgive. But mass murder is hard to forgive. All those lives, all those personalities, those gifts. They were all normal—I was the only anomaly. They didn't have excessive emotions, didn't question anything. They all did their jobs and did them well. Faces flash in my memory. All dead. All murdered. Why would the Designer allow that?

"Thalli?" Diana breaks through my reverie.

I look at this brother and sister. "I apologize."

"Don't apologize." Diana releases a shy smile. "We have had to leave our home too. We understand."

The three of us sit in silence. A bond connects us, a bond of loss and heartache. I do not want to make them relive their hurt. I know they would prefer to forget what happened in Athens, to start over here. But Athens remains a threat, and I need to learn as much as I can about that threat before I walk into it.

"I am going to Athens."

"Yes, Kristie told us." Diana looks at the floor. "You are very brave."

"No." I lace my fingers together. "I am not brave. Believe me. But I do want to help."

"Athens is a dangerous place."

I think again of the house on fire, of Peter being pulled out. The Athenians targeted him, tried to kill him. "Why? Why do they insist on working against us? Don't they see that working together would benefit us all?"

"The king of Athens doesn't want to share his power with anyone. He cares only for his desires, no one else's." Peter lets out a long breath and closes his eyes. There is more to Peter's statement than he is saying. Pain etches his face. Diana's gaze darts from her brother back to the floor, an unspoken something hovering in the air between them.

Diana touches Peter's arm. "Thalli needs to understand how best to infiltrate the palace."

"That is easy." Peter's face relaxes. "All you have to do is tell them you're from the State. The king will be desperate to know what you know."

He speaks after a lengthy silence. "But Athens has intelligent people, good people too. Before the War, our grandparents said there was a large university not far from there. The first king was a professor at that university. But the War destroyed the university and many of those who worked there. The ones who survived, like the first king, were very smart but also very scared."

Diana nods. "Their whole world was dependent on technology. And most of those professors were left without the tools of their trades. All their research, their studies, their inventions—everything was lost. The town survived because they were far enough removed from the effects of the War. But they were not sure how to rebuild without the technology they depended on their whole lives."

"So when our grandparents came, the king immediately brought them into his inner circle." Peter is speaking faster now, his voice stronger. "He wanted them to re-create the technology. He was sure they could reestablish communications with the State, receive aid. But Grandfather refused. He told them if the State knew survivors existed, they would destroy us."

"That is very likely." I nod. "The Scientists believed the old world was beyond help. They created a completely different society. I doubt they would have allowed survivors back into their State."

Diana and Peter look at each other. Diana's eyes close. "I always thought Grandfather was exaggerating."

Peter continues. "The king then decided that if they couldn't connect to the State, they would create their own State. But he was convinced it would be better, stronger. And that one day, they could overcome the State."

"So he convinced your grandparents to help rebuild Athens?"

"Convince?" Peter's laugh is bitter. "The king of Athens

doesn't convince. He commands. He forced my grandparents to help reconstruct the city. Much of the technology that exists got its start from our grandparents—the electricity, the infrastructure. The other citizens took over once it was established."

"The rebuilding took years," Diana says. "Decades, really."

"The city you will see is just a little older than we are." Peter coughs.

"Kristie and Carey said the king focused more on technological development than on food supplies," I say.

"The first king knew that New Hope had also survived the Nuclear War." Diana twists her hands in her lap. "They had sent out groups scouting all around Athens to see what remained. They found New Hope and saw all its fields were still intact."

"Before the War, it had been an agricultural community." Peter nods. "And miraculously the fields survived, as did many of the people."

"So the king decided that rather than spend time and resources trying to create crops in Athens, they would just take New Hope's."

"Didn't the people of New Hope try to fight him?" I can't imagine the original survivors would simply hand over their crops.

"No." Peter sighs. "The king was smart. He told the people here that if they grew the crops, he would supply the technology. He promised they would work together for the 'common good.'"

"But he never meant it." Diana's voice is like steel. "He just wanted to keep them from developing their own technology so he could overpower them."

"Which he did." I think of the fear on the villagers' faces.

"Exactly."

"When the people of New Hope realized the king's true intentions, it was too late." Peter spreads his hands. "Athens, with the help of our grandparents, had grown too powerful to resist."

I shake my head, a question burning in my throat. "But why . . . why would your grandparents agree to help the king? Did they agree with his methods?"

"At first, they were angry enough at the Scientists who remained in New Hope that they cared little for what happened to the people." Regret fills Peter's voice. "But after a while they began to feel bad. They were still upset with the others. But they didn't think it was right to punish the whole village."

"Besides, they had their own plans," Diana said. "They wanted to develop pharmaceuticals to help sick people."

"That was their passion." Peter nods. "They worked on those every spare minute. For years, the king didn't know about that. He was only concerned with them completing the projects he assigned them."

"Electricity and infrastructure?" I ask.

"Right," Peter says. "But when they finally voiced their concern about this village, our father was born." Diana and Peter look at each other, deep pain mirroring in their eyes.

"He threatened their son?"

The muscles in Peter's jaw clench. "The former king and the current king have no problem threatening and destroying anyone who resists them."

"The king demanded that our grandparents continue their work." Diana squeezes her brother's arm. "The city was only halfway built, and he wanted it finished. He also wanted more weapons. When our grandparents refused, he had his guards capture Father. He released him only after our grandparents promised to obey the king's every command. Their opinions were not allowed to be voiced. Guards were placed outside Father's house to ensure they did what they were told and did not attempt escape."

"How old was your father when the guards captured him?"

"Very young." Peter takes a ragged breath. "He never spoke of it, but I know he was terribly mistreated while he was there. The king has no mercy. None."

"Your grandparents had no choice."

"When they finished rebuilding the town, our parents were expecting us," Diana says. "And the new king was in place. This one is even crueler than his father."

"I heard he killed his own father to ascend to the throne," Peter says.

"That's terrible."

"That is King Jason." Peter is so angry his entire face is as red as his eyes.

Diana swallows hard. "When King Jason discovered that our grandparents had developed pharmaceuticals, he insisted they stop and instead develop weapons."

"Using pharmaceuticals?" The thought is terrifying.

"They refused," Diana says. "They could not do it."

Peter's hands clench into fists. "So they killed our mother."

I gasp. "But you were just babies."

"Barely a month old," Diana replies. "And they threatened to kill us too. So our grandparents went to work. They spent years developing all kinds of pharmaceuticals that did many things, but they told the king they hadn't found the right formula for the weapon he wanted."

"The king made sure they wrote down everything they did," Peter says. "And he had his own experts brought in to supervise them. Of course, those 'experts' only knew what our grandparents taught them, so they reported back to the king that they were working on a solution, but their attempts were failing."

"What about your father?" Losing a wife like that had to have been devastating.

"My grandparents taught him enough to make him too valuable to kill, but not enough to allow him to know how to make the weapon."

"He was never the same, though." Diana bites her lip. "Grandfather and Grandmother told us that before our mother died, he was happy and funny, loved life. All we ever knew was a sullen, angry man. I am sure he cared for us, but he was too broken to show it."

"Our grandparents raised us."

"But they never taught us anything about their work." Diana shrugs. "They didn't want us to endure what they had endured."

"They always hoped we could find a way to escape here."

"Did your grandparents help you escape, then?" Hope bubbles in my chest. If Diana and Peter's grandparents are there, they will be allies.

"In a way." A tear slides down Diana's cheek, and the bubble of hope I felt bursts. "The king got tired of waiting for them to complete his project. So he—"

Diana cannot speak. She does not need to, though. "He killed them?"

"He killed them all." Peter spits out the words. "Our grandparents and our father."

"You were spared?" I ask.

"We were forced to watch them die," Diana chokes out through her tears. "They were burned alive, tied to a metal pole. There was no way to stop them."

Burned alive. That is beyond cruel. What kind of king is this? "What did you do?"

"Nothing for a while," Diana says. "We knew we needed to escape, but . . ."

Peter sits up straighter. "But I didn't want to leave."

"What?" I lean forward. "Why?"

"Helen." The one word is almost a sigh. I recognize the look in his eye.

"You loved her."

"I love her." Peter closes his eyes.

"Why not bring her with you? Escape together?"

"It isn't that simple."

"Does she love you?"

"Yes."

"Then what is it?"

"Helen is the king's daughter."

CHAPTER TWENTY-TWO

allow this news to sink into my brain. Peter is in love with the king's daughter. The king who murdered his parents and grandparents. "How?"

Peter shrugs. "I don't want to talk about it. And you must not let anyone know you know this. When the king discovered we wished to be together, he decreed my death. Helen found out and risked her life to help me escape."

"How did you do it?"

"I climbed out on the roof of one of the factories. Helen tied sheets together so I could scale down the city walls. It was late at night. It's a miracle the guards didn't see me. But I made it."

"What about you?" I look at Diana. "What did they do to you when they found out?"

"Nothing." Diana stares out the window. "They knew I had nothing left. There was nothing to be gained from hurting or killing me. Not until Peter was found."

"They were sure they would get me back," Peter says. "And when they did, then they would have hurt her. To punish me. So I knew I couldn't get caught. I would not allow Diana to suffer for me. I was going to keep going, but the folks here told me there was nowhere else to go and that Athens would attack whether I was here or not. A few of them weren't happy I was here. But most of the people made me feel welcome. So I stayed, and I hoped that the king would let it go. It was a stupid hope."

"I kept working at the factory where I worked for the last year." Diana looks at me. "No one spoke to me. It was like I had a disease. But no one touched me either. For that, I am thankful."

"But then you discovered the plan to attack New Hope and retrieve your brother?" I recall her story, hiding in the back of a car the soldiers drove here from Athens.

"Yes."

"They'll just come again." I see now why the villagers are so upset. But they have no right to be upset at these two. They are innocent. Staying in Athens would have been a death sentence.

"They won't stop until someone stops them," Peter says.

This is what Carey and Kristie said. But I do not feel any closer to comprehending how to stop them now than I did before I came in.

"Be careful in there," Diana says.

"You can't trust anyone." Peter leans forward. "They may act friendly, but they're all master deceivers. You can't imagine the things that have been done to the people of Athens. *They* can't imagine. Most of the citizens are completely fooled. I think they are drugged."

"Drugged?"

"Yes, the people who worked with my grandparents learned enough to make mind-altering pharmaceuticals." Peter shakes his head. "I am sure the people there are drugged."

"Or just frightened." Diana places her hand on Peter's.

"Whatever the case, you will find no allies there."

"What about Helen?"

"Don't bring her into this." Peter takes in a shaky breath. "She has been through enough."

There is more that Peter and Diana are not telling me. About Helen. But I do not ask. I'm sure that information is not necessary to know in order to help New Hope. And I'm also sure that information is painful, both to Peter and to Helen. Some secrets are best left unsaid.

"One asset you have is you're from the State," Diana says.

"Yes." Peter's eyes brighten. "They have been waiting thirty-five years for someone to escape from the State, the way our grandparents did."

"They never learned how to communicate outside of our town. The king wants very much to know what the State knows, things my grandparents didn't tell them." Diana nods.

"But I don't know about technology." I regret, once again, not paying attention to my lessons on the learning pad. Should I let Rhen go in my place? I shake that thought immediately. She is needed here. I am the most expendable of the escapees. "I am a Musician."

"You need to make them believe you know more than you

do, then," Peter says. "If they find you useless, you will end up like my grandparents. They need to see you as valuable."

"But they'll find out I am not."

"You know more than you think," Diana assures me. "You were raised in the State. You have been surrounded by technology Athens is desperate to have."

Diana is right. "I spent the last few months inside the Scientists' Quarters. I was tested for all sorts of things. I saw some of what they were looking for, what they were using."

"Perfect!" Diana claps her hands. "Tell them about it. Tell them everything you recall. Make yourself sound brilliant."

I sigh. Now I truly wish it were Rhen going. Or Berk. He actually could tell them what they want to know. But that, of course, is exactly why they shouldn't go. These people do not need to know what the Scientists know. This king sounds as evil as Dr. Loudin, as destructive. The more ignorant he remains, the better for everyone.

"But what do I do?" I ask. "How do I help New Hope?"

"Earn the king's trust," Peter says. "He will never choose to have peace with New Hope. But if he can be convinced that it is in his best interest to be at peace, then he might leave us alone."

"How do I convince him of that?" This is the same man who kills people who don't do what he says, whose father taught him that New Hope was to be conquered. How do I combat that?

Peter looks at Diana. "That, I don't know."

"But you found a way to escape from the State." Diana smiles. "This should be easy compared to that."

Somehow, this encouragement does not help me. I leave the room, thanking the siblings, even more frightened about this task I have chosen to undertake.

CHAPTER TWENTY-THREE

have something for you." John has taken me for a walk to the nearest pond. John loves to be near water. He pulls out a wrinkled sheet of paper. It has writing on it. I can barely read what it says.

"What is this?"

"Psalm 23." John looks out over the pond as he speaks, reciting the words from memory. "'The LORD is my shepherd; I shall not want. He makes me to lie down in green pastures; He leads me beside the still waters. He restores my soul; He leads me in the paths of righteousness for His name's sake.'"

The words settle deep into my heart in a way no other words

ever have. I feel as if this was written just for me. John takes my hand in his as he continues. "'Yea, though I walk through the valley of the shadow of death, I will fear no evil; for You are with me; Your rod and Your staff, they comfort me. You prepare a table before me in the presence of my enemies; You anoint my head with oil; my cup runs over. Surely goodness and mercy shall follow me all the days of my life; and I will dwell in the house of the LORD forever.'"

We are silent. I look at the pond, the green grass that surrounds it. "I will fear no evil."

John squeezes my hand. "It is when we walk through the darkest valleys that we sense the Designer with us most strongly."

"So how do I do it?" I permit myself to feel the fear I have been hiding from the others. "How do I not fear evil?"

John folds the paper and closes it in my hands. "You think on these words, not on the fear. Let the Designer comfort you. Let him prepare a table for you in the presence of your enemies."

I hug John. He has lost weight in the weeks since we left the State. But he is strong in ways I will never be. I pray I can know the Designer like he does, have the faith he has.

"Looks like you have another visitor." John pulls away and points behind me. Berk is walking up. He does not speak until John is far enough away he will not hear our conversation.

"Are you sure you want to do this?"

Berk has not spoken to me in two weeks, and this is how he breaks the silence? I want to scoop up the muddy earth at my feet and throw it at him. But I squeeze the paper in my hand, remind myself of what John taught me, of the peace I felt when I was with him.

"I have to do it."

"Why?"

"This is our home now." I wave my arms toward the village.

"But what if something happens to you?"

"Like you really care."

Berk takes a step back. He closes his eyes and sucks in a loud breath. "When will you let this go, Thalli?"

I stare back at him, wanting to say so much but unable to allow even one word to pass through my lips.

"You have to let me go." Berk looks at me, his pupils so wide the green around them is a thin line. "I know more about what the Scientists have been working on."

"That's why you can't go." I fold my arms tight against my chest. "You know too much. You would be forced to help them accomplish what they cannot be allowed to accomplish."

"I wouldn't need to tell them everything. Just enough to prove I know what I am doing. Like Peter and Diana's grandparents. They never used what they knew to develop the weapon the king wanted."

"And they were killed for it."

"After how many years, Thalli?" Berk's voice is louder now. "I won't be there that long."

"I am going." I look at Berk. His pupils are smaller now. I see the gold flecks in his eyes and want nothing more than to lose myself there, to forget this task.

"Why not let Rhen go?"

"Rhen doesn't question authority. Not much, anyway. I question everything. And for this particular job, that is a good trait. I will dig into as much about Athens as I can. I won't even have to try. I'm already asking a hundred questions in my head.

I had to stop myself with Peter and Diana. I could have spent a week in there, delving into their memories, finding out every last particle of information there is to find. But I cannot put off going to Athens any longer. They need to be stopped now. And I am the best option for stopping them."

"But if they find out who you are . . ."

"I will do my best to make sure that doesn't happen."

Berk runs a hand through his brown hair. "But you can't be sure. They could kill you as soon as you walk up to the gate."

"And they could kill you before I get there too." I take a step closer to Berk, place my hand over his heart. I feel it beating, feel the connection that no amount of time or frustration or jealousy could ever completely dissolve. "I need to do this."

"You *think* you need to do this." Berk places his hand over mine. "You're trying to protect us, Thalli. To save us. But you don't need to do that."

I stare into Berk's eyes. "Of course I do. New Hope is in danger and someone needs to go to Athens to try to help them. You are sick, John is old, Rhen is needed here."

"No." Berk pulls me to him, crushing me in his embrace.

"You are not thinking logically." I am speaking more to myself than to him. "You're thinking with your heart."

Berk's mouth is at my ear, his breath warming my neck, my heart, softening my resolve. "Of course I'm thinking with my heart. You have my heart."

I want to stay, to forget what we have planned. But I cannot. I will not allow Berk to keep me from doing what must be done. I cannot leave New Hope exposed, cannot allow any more damage to be done here. I pull myself from his embrace. I will my heart to turn back to ice, rebuild the wall between him and me.

He will not understand, but it is for the best. This is bigger than us, more important.

"Then I give it back to you, Berk. I don't want your heart." I don't want to look at him, don't want to watch his face drop, his eyes cloud over with pain. But I cannot bring myself to look away. Not when this might be the last time I see his face. "Give it to someone who won't hurt it. Because I cannot make that promise."

He opens his mouth, but nothing comes out. I turn away from Berk and run as fast and as far as I can.

CHAPTER TWENTY-FOUR

Carey was able to fix the transport, so I am flying to Athens, not walking. I should be rehearsing my story as I go, but my mind will not focus. I think of the village I left behind. Of John and Rhen.

I refuse to let myself think of Berk. Of him looking at me, of the hurt in his eyes. Of me turning away, not speaking. I know it was best. I do not know how long I will be gone, what will happen to me. Berk deserves more than what I can give him. But knowing I made the right decision does not make it any less painful.

I think of the land that stretches out green and beautiful,

then turns suddenly brown and dead. No life, no growth. Not the ashy gray I saw coming down here, but lifeless just the same. I think of where I am going and what I am to do.

John told me the story of two spies who were sent into an enemy's land. A woman named Rahab hid them and lied for them, and eventually the spies escaped, with Rahab, and the enemy's city was captured by those who worshipped the Designer.

Lying is wrong. Yet here I am, again preparing to lie to others. Last time, I lied about a surgery Dr. Loudin performed. Pretended my memory was erased so my life would be spared. I felt the same struggle then that I do now. But now, a whole village is depending on me.

I know the Designer is leading me into this valley of the shadow of death. But is he asking me to lie, the way the spies asked Rahab to lie? Or am I doing it because I think it's the only way? And what if I don't lie? What if I tell them the truth—I am from the State, my friends are in New Hope, and we want peace? But if they are the type of people Peter and Diana say they are, then that admission could cause greater harm to befall my friends in New Hope.

I am so conflicted. I want to do what is right. And the others have advised me that in this case, lying about my true motives is best for everyone involved. But isn't there some way to be honest and still protect the village?

I don't have any more time to think. On the horizon, I see a fortress. Athens.

The wall isn't what I expected. It is not made from the trees the homes in New Hope are made of. It looks man-made but solid. It is black and it is tall. Very tall. The land here is much flatter than New Hope, so I can see the whole shape—a large square. Because I am on the transport, I can see inside the structure. There are many homes, all square, all black. They are evenly spaced apart. This village was created after the War, not rebuilt from homes that survived, like New Hope. The whole layout is far too organized for it to have been from the previous era.

There are very few plots of green land. Unlike New Hope, which is mostly green with relatively few houses among it. There is a fenced-in area where the cows that I assume were stolen from New Hope reside. Smoke rises from several facilities, but not like the smoke that came out of the house in New Hope. This is controlled smoke. It is dark, almost black, and smells of chemicals. As I get closer I see part of the wall open and someone ride out on a horse. The rider is coming toward me, waving me down.

I ease the transport to the ground and step off. I wave a greeting. I do not want to show fear. I should show relief—after traveling for so long, I have finally found life. I repeat the words of the psalm John gave me as I walk forward.

His face covered by a black fabric, the rider has stopped, but he is still on his horse. When he speaks, his voice is slightly muffled. "Where are you from?"

"I escaped the State."

The rider pulls the fabric off his face. His hair is long, almost to his shoulders, and is a light color—almost as blond as Rhen's. It curls, though, unlike Rhen's straight hair. His face is tan, and as he steps closer, I see that his eyes are a light blue. The color of the sky in the morning. He is young. Not much older than I am, but he carries himself like one with authority.

"No one has escaped the State in almost forty years." His eyes narrow.

"How do you know?"

"How do I know you are from the State?"

The rider is just a few feet from me now. He has stopped moving, but his eyes drill into mine. I force myself to return his gaze. I will not be intimidated. "I travel hundreds of miles to be free from tyrannical rule, and this is what I find? If you will not accept me, please direct me to a place that will."

The rider's mouth relaxes slightly. He might be smiling, but his gaze is still so severe, I am not sure. "I am Alex. Prince of Athens. I apologize for the welcome. But we have to be careful."

"I am Thalli, Alex." I nod toward him, this prince, and try not to reveal my distrust. This is the king's son—the king who killed Peter and Diana's family. But it is Helen's brother. Who is he more like?

"Why did you escape the State?"

"The Scientists wanted to kill me."

Alex laughs, but it is not a pleasant sound. "And why would they want to kill someone as pretty as you?" He steps closer. I can see dark eyelashes framing his sky-blue eyes and light eyebrows raised slightly as he appraises me.

"I am too emotional."

"Too emotional?" Alex's eyebrows rise more. "That is a crime worthy of death in the State, is it?"

"Yes."

"Everyone in the State has an occupation, correct?" His face relaxes, but his gaze is still trained on me.

I am surprised at this change of topic, but I remain calm, answering him in the same tone. "Correct."

"And what was yours?"

"I was the pod Musician."

"Musician?" Alex places his hands on his hips. "I was hoping you'd be an expert in something a little more useful."

"Music aids everyone in being more productive." I step forward. "It increases brain activity and potential. It provides a tranquil atmosphere. Music is incredibly useful for any civilized society."

Alex laughs again. "I see why they found you to be too emotional."

I step back again. I need to control myself. I also need to be useful to him. I think back on what Peter and Diana said. "I studied with the Scientists, though. I spent significant time in their quarters, working with them on new developments." Does *not* telling the whole truth count as a lie?

"That sounds very interesting."

"I would be happy to tell you all about it."

"In exchange for what?" Alex's blue eyes have yet to leave mine. I try to maintain the stare, maintain my story, and maintain my composure, but I am finding it increasingly difficult.

"I would like to be part of your village."

"We are not a village." Alex's eyes harden. "We are Athens."

"I'm sorry. I did not mean to offend."

"I believe you." He responds like a Scientist. Perhaps royalty and Scientists are the same thing in Athens. "Come with me. My father will, no doubt, wish to learn more about the State."

"Of course."

Alex's gaze lands on the transport. Curiosity replaces the haughtiness in his eyes.

"Would you like to ride with me?"

I think I see a bit of fear on Alex's face, but it is quickly masked. "I need to return with my horse. Perhaps another time, though."

I bite my lip to keep from laughing. Prince Alex is afraid of my transport. He climbs back on his horse and points it toward the towering walls of Athens.

I have arrived.

CHAPTER TWENTY-FIVE

M y father was a history professor." King Jason's voice is deep, like a tuba. I barely hear what he is saying, I am so enthralled by the tone of his voice. "A leading scholar on ancient Greece. When the War destroyed everything, he thought ours was the only surviving village. He gathered the leaders together and insisted we start over, create here a new Athens. A world power. He was chosen to be king and established the laws of our land. When he died, I replaced him."

I vaguely recall reading about this ancient Greece, about monarchies and such, but I dare not make him aware of how little I comprehend. "This is a beautiful state."

"We have worked hard to make it so." The king's bass voice echoes through the large room. "We have striven to create new technologies, not to re-create the old. We hope to one day join with the State below. Perhaps you can aid us in that."

My heartbeat quickens. My greatest fear is being returned to the State. "I am a fugitive from the State."

"They wanted to kill her because she was too emotional." Alex stands beside his father. He is smiling as he speaks.

"Too emotional?" The king's smile is like his son's, though his eyes aren't as light a blue as Alex's. His hair, though, is a darker blond, cut short, and receding. "We here in Athens embrace emotions. We do not fear them. Right, son?"

"Certainly, Father." Some unspoken idea passes between them before the king continues.

"We do not want to overwhelm you on your first day here." The king motions to Alex. "Take Thalli to our guest room. After you've a good night's rest, Alex will show you around our fair city."

"I would very much like to see it now, if that's all right." The thought of going to sleep is impossible.

"As you wish." The king passes another unspoken message along to his son. "Show her around, Alex. The grand tour. It isn't often we have a visitor from the State."

Alex opens the door out of what he calls the "grand hall." I am glad to be out. This palace is overly ornate—though the outside of all the buildings is black, inside there are more colors than would be necessary in twenty houses. Gold seems to be a favorite, in the grand hall especially. There are columns in gold, paintings framed in gold, and the whole chair where the king sat was of gold. Not actual gold, I am sure.

That element couldn't be found here in that abundance. But the citizens obviously found a way to reproduce it in a paint or a covering.

"We live in the palace," Alex says as he leads me up a staircase with a rail covered in—what else?—gold. "My father, my sister, and me."

I want to meet Helen, to ask about her. To tell her Peter is all right. But I am not supposed to know anything about her. I have to maintain my story as a fugitive arriving from the State. A fugitive who knows no one in and nothing about New Hope. "And your mother?"

Alex slows down for a moment but then moves on. "She died five years ago."

"I'm sorry." I wait to see if he will elaborate, but he does not.

We reach the top of the stairs, and it leads down a hallway with three doors on each side. "These are the bedrooms. My father has his own suite one floor above, but my sister and I both sleep here. I'm the last room on the right. Helen is across from me. You will stay here, in this first room."

Alex opens the door and I look in. The room is very large and colorful. Red seems to be the color of choice in here, with the bed covering, the window coverings, and the floor coverings all in the same scarlet shade. But the fabric is different. I walk to the window and touch it. It is soft, but not like the material used in New Hope and certainly not what we had in the State. "What is this?"

"Do you like it?" Alex is behind me. Closer than I would like. If I turn, we would almost be touching. He smells nice, a different sort of smell than anything I've encountered before. He reaches past my shoulder to touch the fabric, grazing my arm with his. "We develop that material here. It is synthetic silk. I'll show you the factory later."

"That would be wonderful."

Alex finally moves away, and I rush out of the room. His nearness is disconcerting. His kindness is baffling. What did his father say to Alex to make him so attentive? What were the unspoken messages being sent? I expected to be an oddity, coming from the State. And I knew they would want to know more about what is going on there. But they aren't asking me questions. Alex is giving me a tour and standing close. The king remains in his chamber. Of all the scenarios I imagined, this was not one of them.

I look to my right. There is another set of stairs at the end of the hallway, leading up to the king's suite or down into the kitchen. We go down. As we descend, something smells wonderful. My stomach growls as soon as we reach the last step.

"Would you like some lunch?" Alex snaps his fingers and a woman stirring a pot at a cooking appliance quickly turns. Her eyes look almost empty.

"Yes, Prince Alex? What can I do for you?"

"My guest is hungry."

The woman lowers her head and opens a door that leads to a storage room. She comes out with a plate, silverware, and a cup. She fills the plate with the contents of the pot she was stirring. She walks with it into an adjoining room. Alex follows her in and seats me at a long table. It is gold and filled with bowls of fruit and candles, and covered with a cloth made out of the same material I saw in the bedroom. The plate is decorated all along the edges. I touch the designs. I have never seen anything like it.

"We make those too." Alex smiles as the woman places a drink in front of me. The cup has a design that mirrors that of the plate.

"Beautiful."

"What do you use in the State?"

Now he asks questions. I want to begin eating—the food smells delicious, even though I have no idea what is in it—but I explain how everything in the State is white. The food is genetically engineered to provide us with the nutrients we need.

"But how does it taste?"

"Taste?" I think of the meals we shared in Pod C. "I never thought about it."

"Then it must not be very good." Alex turns to face me. "Try this and tell me what you think."

I take a forkful of the meal and place it in my mouth. My mouth waters and I close my eyes with the pleasure of it. "Wonderful."

"I'm glad you like it." Alex smiles.

He really has a kind face. Perhaps he is more like his sister than his father. I want to ask him about himself. I find the process of learning about a person fascinating; something I have only recently been able to do. In the State, I knew everyone since birth. There was no need to ask them any questions. I knew all the answers. And this . . . this prince—raised by a king in a world totally different from John's or mine, totally different from New Hope. I want to know everything about him—his past, his memories. But I hold back. I am not here to get to know Alex. I am here to find out about Athens. But couldn't I do both?

I stop thinking because I need to concentrate on what I am eating. Flavors are bursting on my tongue, even after I swallow.

I want to enjoy the sensations. I don't recall the food in New Hope tasting this good.

Alex is watching me. One trait that is the same from the outside here is his stare. He watches everything I do. But it isn't quite as uncomfortable as I thought. In fact, I might like it. I need a friend here, an ally. Maybe Alex could be that. And if he could be, there is hope. He is heir to the throne. He doesn't seem the type to burn someone alive or try to destroy innocent villagers.

Of course, I have been fooled before. I need to spend more time with him before I consider trusting this young man.

I take the last bite of the food with reluctance. "This was the best thing I have ever tasted."

"This was a simple dish." Alex's blue eyes twinkle in the lamplight. "Wait until you try some of our gourmet dishes."

"I can't wait." That is one whole truth I can gladly state.

"There's much more of the palace to see." Alex stands.

"I don't know if I have the energy to see more right now." Just standing made me tired. "I just want to sleep. Is that all right?"

"Of course. That is the sign of a good meal."

I walk back to my room, still savoring the taste of the food. Perhaps Athens isn't as terrible a place as I was led to believe. I fall into the bed covered in synthetic silk and dream of breakfast.

CHAPTER TWENTY-SIX

A week has gone by. It has taken that long for me to see all of Athens.

The day after I arrived I toured the rest of the palace. And I ate steak and potatoes and asparagus, all flavored with different spices. All delicious. The palace is ornate and massive and unlike anything in the State. It was built from stones quarried not far from here, natural stone. Most of the furniture and appliances are made from synthetic materials, but none of those materials are similar to what was made in the State. They were all made here. I asked who helped develop them—knowing the answer—but Alex only responds that it was "the people."

Then he took me to see what the people do—we spent the last few days touring factories that make everything from utensils to vehicles. Everyone works without complaint. They all seemed happy to see Alex. And Alex was happy to see them. He is kind to everyone. Authoritative but kind. He knows the names of many people. I cannot even try to recall all the names I heard. They are so strange, names like Abraham and Katherine and Nicholas. I have difficulty even pronouncing them.

These Athenians do not seem at all like the evil people Peter and Diana painted them to be. They work hard and laugh and seem to enjoy their lives. I saw some last night, singing and eating at what Alex called a restaurant, playing games at large tables. They didn't appear to be worried that they would be destroyed by a brutal king or plotting the deaths of innocent people in the nearby village.

I am feeling more and more confident that Alex could be an ally in brokering peace with New Hope. He seems to want what is best for the people of Athens. He wants them to be happy and successful. He is very concerned for my welfare too, always asking if I slept well, if I liked my food, if there is anything more I need.

The king calls me to his chambers every day. He asks many questions about the State—what I learned, how I was taught, what the Scientists were doing. I answer as much as I can to demonstrate a thorough knowledge. I try not to speak too much of Berk and Rhen. Nothing of John. I told them I escaped alone. The kinder they are to me, the more guilt I feel at deceiving them. But if I am right and they are better than those in New Hope believe, then maybe I can reveal the truth in time.

I recall my conversation with Peter and Diana, the fear and

anger in their eyes. I recall seeing a group from Athens riding toward New Hope, to take their food and set fire to their homes. What I am seeing now and what I saw then are paradoxical. I must determine the truth before I can move on.

"I have a surprise for you today." Alex stands outside my door. He is wearing a purple shirt and brown pants, a departure from his usual black.

"A surprise?" I follow Alex down the stairs that lead through the grand hall to the heavy door at the palace entrance.

It is warm outside, and I am grateful for the dress Helen loaned me. I don't see her often. I feel a connection to her because of what Peter said. But Alex says she rarely leaves her room. "Depressed" he called it. I tried to press him for more information about his sister, but he responded in much the same way as he did when I asked him about his mother: with complete silence.

But Helen did bring a box full of clothes to my room three days ago. Clothes like this dress, made out of the synthetic silk. It feels cool against my skin. I find it strange to have my legs bare, but I can learn to enjoy this sensation. I wish Helen would have stayed and talked to me. She left the box outside my room, knocked, and was gone by the time I opened the door.

The walkways here are narrow. So much of the space is filled with buildings—some homes, many factories. Very little food is grown or raised here. When I asked Alex about that, he simply said they have outside sources for that. I want to ask him more about that. Those "outside sources" are the people of New Hope. I want to tell him those people work hard to raise their crops, that they don't deserve to have their crops taken from them, that they could combine their resources and be two strong communities at peace instead of two separate, warring communities.

But I don't say any of that because the time is not right. And because Alex is talking and I am supposed to be listening, learning more about this city.

We pass the largest building—their medical facility. Alex told me they are most proud of their pharmaceuticals. I tried to mock surprise when he said two of the Scientists from the State escaped here not long after the War. He said they were able to develop vaccines for the children and medicine for the sick. So much good has been done here. Peter and Diana did not mention any of that. Maybe they didn't know.

"Here it is." The building, like all the others, is coated in black. Solar power in Athens is infused in the black paint, allowing the entire city to have electricity and maintain the factories. An ingenious device, actually, using space that is already available to serve a dual purpose.

He opens the door of a small building. Dust fills my nostrils. This is obviously used very little. He turns the knob for the light panels, and I see piles of dusty instruments. Clarinets and oboes and saxophones. I want to jump up and shout when I see a violin on its side in the far corner of the room.

"I remember you said you were a Musician in the State," Alex says. "We haven't used this building for years—we've been too focused on other tasks. But you are welcome to choose as many instruments as you want, and we will have them sent back to the palace for you to play anytime."

I put my hand over my chest. I cannot speak. My eyes feel like my stomach the first day I was here—starving, with a delicious feast set before me.

"I have to visit one of the factories." Alex is speaking, but I barely hear him. "I will leave you here. Can you find your way back to the palace when you're done?"

I think I want to move my room here, stay for days, weeks, and never come out. But I just nod at Alex, my mind filling with music.

"You're happy here, aren't you?" Something in his tone pulls me back to this room.

"Of course." I look into his eyes, making sure he understands how sincerely I feel this. "Happier than I have been in a long time."

Another look passes over Alex's face. I don't know what it is, but the thrill at being with so many instruments keeps me from being able to think about it.

Alex shuts the door, and I rush to the violin. It is coated with dust. I open a cabinet and find cleaning cloths and sheets of music. Somewhere in the history of Athens, someone loved music. I can bring that love back.

I rub the cloth into the wood, clean the strings, tighten them, and find a bow in decent enough shape to use. My heart aches with longing to play. I lift the instrument to my chin, lay the bow on the strings, and play all I have been feeling since we arrived here.

I find my memories of New Hope are fuzzy. I can't even recall the emotion of traveling from the State to get there. I remember seeing Alex greet me outside Athens. His friendly smile, his helpfulness. The kindness of the king. This is a wonderful place, and I am fortunate to be here.

141

CHAPTER TWENTY-SEVEN

am playing the piano when Alex returns. The instrument is terribly out of tune, but I enjoy the feel of the keys beneath my fingers anyway.

"You play beautifully." Alex pulls a chair next to me. "Please don't stop. I have never heard piano playing before."

"How can you have all these instruments and allow them to sit and collect dust?" I talk as I play. Alex is watching my fingers.

"After the War my grandfather insisted the people of Athens focus on building the factories." Alex leans back in his chair as I transition to another song. "He wanted our city to be firmly established. Then the wall needed to be constructed, our forces needed to be trained . . ."

"Forces?" I stop playing.

"We have enemies."

"But the War?" I'm not sure how much I should reveal.

"Ours wasn't the only group of survivors. There is another, smaller village about sixty miles away."

"Why don't you work together?" I try to keep my voice as even as possible. Curious, not demanding. "Why must you be enemies?"

Alex shrugs, his blue eyes looking deep into mine. "They do not wish to work with us."

I bite back an argument. Are they really trying? I saw no evidence that New Hope had animosity toward Athens. But all I heard was their perspective. Perhaps there is more going on. I cannot rid myself of this feeling that the people of Athens are better than what those in New Hope believe.

"So how did you learn to play so well?"

"I was designed to play well."

"Designed?" Alex says the word like he has never heard it before. It is easy to forget what different beginnings we have had.

"You say there were Scientists here who escaped the State." I play again. I can speak with greater freedom when I am playing than when I have nothing to do but look at Alex. "Did they not speak of their work?"

"I did not know the Scientists well. But what does that have to do with anything?"

I sigh. This is a strange discussion. I begin playing again, modifying the key of the piece to reflect this. Alex laughs. It is a nice sound. "I do not have parents."

"What?" Alex jumps up. I keep playing and he eventually returns to his seat.

"The Scientists believed that the ancient way of procreating was detrimental to the evolution of the human species. So they eliminated it."

"But how—?" This is the first time I have ever seen Alex anything but confident.

"The ingredients to create life were stored in the State years before the War. The Scientists use those ingredients to develop embryos. The Geneticists then inject the embryos with the genes they will need to be of most use to the State." I repeat what I was taught in so many lessons. "Each member of each pod has a role to fill. Each role is important, each individual is important, and we all must work together to maintain peace and unity in the State."

"So you were . . . made?"

I think of the Designer, of how John told me we are his creations. He created the ingredients for life. The Scientists might manipulate them, but that does not make us any less his. But I do not feel the freedom to say that to Alex yet. "I was designed to be a Musician."

"So you were just born knowing how to play like that?"

It is my turn to laugh. "No. I had to take lessons and practice. But I have the intellect and gifting to be able to learn quickly and retain well."

"Did you enjoy living there?"

"That is a difficult question." So many memories flood my mind. "It was all I knew, so in that respect I enjoyed it. I was able to play instruments almost every day, and I enjoyed that very much."

"But...?"

"But I was very different." I think of the many times I was corrected for my behavior, of how I always felt out of place.

"In what way?"

"I was an anomaly." Even now, even with all I have learned, admitting that is difficult. "We were designed without the excessive emotions the Scientists believed were harmful."

"I do recall my father discussing that with me." Alex leans forward. "But he disagreed with the Scientists. He thinks emotions are very good. Necessary, even."

I swallow hard. Alex is so close to me, I can feel his breath on my face. I lean back. "I was to be annihilated because of mine."

"Annihilated?" Alex's voice rises. He certainly has no problem expressing emotions. "That is ridiculous."

"That is why I escaped."

"I'm glad you did." There is something I cannot identify in Alex's eyes. Almost like he's sad. But then it passes, and he is confident again. "I think you will find you are most welcome here in Athens."

"Thank you." I smile. "I feel most welcome."

"And you like it here?" Again, there is that strange look.

"Very much."

Alex sighs and places his palm against my cheek. Its warmth radiates through my whole body. "I'm glad you are here too. You are amazing."

I do not know how to respond to this. And I realize we have done nothing but talk about me. I want to learn more about Athens, more about Alex, but he tells me we must go. The king is having a dinner party tonight, and I am invited. It is a special occasion, though Alex won't tell me what, exactly. He wants me to be surprised.

We weave through the streets in silence. Alex is moving faster than normal. He seems disturbed, though I don't know why.

When I return to my room, a beautiful dress is laid out on my sleeping platform. It is longer than the one I am wearing. It is a rich green color, with long sleeves and a full skirt.

A woman comes in to fix my hair. Her utensils are very hot, cylindrical, and they transform my hair into curls that hang down on my shoulders and bounce when I walk. I look in the mirror, and I can hardly believe I am looking at myself. The woman applied colors to my cheeks and lips, a pencil to my eyelids. I look like pictures of the ancients I saw on my learning pad so long ago.

"This perfume has been made especially for you." The woman sprays my face with the strong-smelling substance, and I cough in an attempt to dispel it from my mouth. It smells familiar, though. This has been sprayed in my room perhaps, or worn by someone near me. It cannot have been made especially for me. But I will not argue.

Then I am walking down into the main hall. It has been transformed. It is lit with candles, tables cover the floor, women in beautiful gowns linger by the tables with men who are equally elegant.

"You look beautiful." Alex is at the bottom of the stairs. I did not even notice him move to meet me. He is dressed like all the other men—black pants, white shirt, black jacket. He, however, has nothing around his neck. His hair is combed back and held with a tie. I like it better when his hair isn't combed down.

I step closer to him and am overwhelmed with the thought of how handsome he is. I feel a little guilty for thinking that somehow. My head feels foggy, perhaps from the crowd or the perfume or the exhaustion of playing instruments all afternoon.

"My father would like you to sit at the table with us." Alex places my hand on his arm, and we walk toward the table on the raised platform at the front of the room. Helen is there, looking sad. She speaks to me, but she does not look at me.

"It's lovely, isn't it?" Her voice is deeper than the voices of most girls I know, but it's pleasant and smooth. "Lovely people, lovely food, lovely occasion."

I want to ask what the occasion is, and why she is so morose about it. I want to whisper to her that Peter loves her and he is fine. I want to see her smile, to do something to help her recover from her depression. I try to begin a conversation with Helen, but I am stopped by the king clinking a fork against his glass. The people are quickly quiet, all eyes on the king who is standing.

"Ladies and gentlemen, thank you all for coming to this very special evening." Though his words are formal and his tone is kind, his eyes seem firm and somewhat predatory. It is a bit unnerving. "I am pleased to announce tonight the engagement of my son, Alex."

I try not to gasp as I recall the word *engagement*. Alex has been with me so much the last week and I'm surprised he has not told me about this. John spoke of his engagement to Amy, how they planned what they called a wedding, and how exciting it all was.

"I have chosen a wife for my son whom I feel confident will be an asset to his future role as king."

All eyes are on us, our table, sharing smiles and nods. I look around. Where is the fiancée? Perhaps it is their custom to have the bride-to-be enter after the announcement is made.

"Thalli, please stand." The king motions me up, but I cannot move. Surely he does not mean—Alex stands and pulls me up beside him.

"Citizens of Athens. Meet your future queen."

CHAPTER TWENTY-EIGHT

People are clapping and Alex is hugging me and the king is laughing genially. I am frozen. The fog that my mind was in has lifted, and I am suddenly, painfully aware that this cannot be. I will not embarrass the king or Alex by refusing at this dinner. Planned for me. And Alex. And our engagement.

How did this happen? Why would such an announcement be made without even consulting me? That is State-like behavior. Not the actions of a place that allows for freedom and emotion. Surely there has been a mistake. Or perhaps engagement means something different here than what John spoke of.

I release a breath I did not realize I had been holding. Of course that's what it is. I will ask Alex afterward how they define it. We will laugh over my misunderstanding.

We sit and begin our meal. Music is playing. "I thought you said there were no instruments here," I say to Alex as a delicious-smelling liquid is placed in front of us. Alex sips it with a spoon, so I do the same.

Alex looks at me, his brows coming together. "I didn't think that would be the first question you asked me."

"I'm saving the others for when we are not surrounded by dozens of people." I smile. "The music?"

"Right." He points to a box above our heads. "It is a recording, from before. We have some specialists who restored all the recordings the people of Athens had. We play them only on special occasions. Like this. Do you like it?"

There are several instruments playing at once. I love the sound. "It is beautiful."

The rest of the evening goes by in a blur. I cannot focus, cannot even think of the questions I want to ask. Alex is kind and attentive and very handsome. I would not mind if the Athenian definition of *engagement* is the same as the other one I have heard. Although I cannot seem to remember where I heard that other one. Nothing seems to be real except Alex and the king and this food and the party.

The king stands again, after we have eaten a food made from apples and sugar. My stomach is too full to hold any more food, so I hope he isn't announcing that more is on its way.

"Thank you all for coming." He motions to the doors, which are being opened by the men who work here. "We will invite you all back for the wedding."

The people clap and walk out. They do not talk as they exit. They simply leave, filing out one at a time, very orderly.

Wedding... I know the word *wedding*, and I know the word *engagement*, though I still don't recall how I know them. When the king made the announcement, he said I was their future queen. Engagement. Wedding. Queen. And I am struck with an uncomfortable reality.

The woman who fixed my hair walks by, and I smell "my" perfume again. I keep my mouth closed but breathe it in. It is a pleasant scent. I feel myself relaxing, perhaps because the people are gone and it is quieter. I look around the table. Alex and I are the only ones left. I barely recall seeing the others leave. This food is making me tired, I suppose. They eat so much more than I am used to eating.

"How are you feeling?" Alex looks at me, and I am struck with how very blue his eyes are. He is handsome. So handsome. And he always seems to look at me like I am something special, treasured. I realize I am staring at him when I should be answering him, and I am ashamed.

"I feel wonderful." I mean it. I don't recall ever feeling this good. "Did you put something in that food to make me feel this good?"

Alex stands up, his smile gone. "Why would you ask that?"

I stand and place a hand on his arm. "It was a joke. You enjoy jokes, right?"

"Of course." He relaxes, but for once, his eyes are not looking at me. They are staring off into the distance. I miss his gaze.

"I do have a question." We are walking out of the hall, then up the stairs. I like the feel of Alex's hand in mine. "We are engaged?"

"Yes."

"And that means we will get married?"

Alex stops on the stair and looks at me. "Yes."

I try to pull up a memory. It feels like it is hidden in my brain, miles away. "Do you love me?"

Alex looks at me for a long time, then he reaches to replace a strand of curled hair into the clip that was holding it. "I think you are one of the most interesting, beautiful, fascinating people I have ever known."

"You didn't answer my question."

"Do I love you?" His gaze moves from my eyes to my lips and back again. "I have feelings for you I've never had for anyone else."

"Feelings aren't love."

"Why does it matter? We're a good match. I will take care of you."

"But you shouldn't marry me if you don't love me." I don't know how I know that, but I feel the truth of the statement as soon as it comes out of my mouth. "And I don't know if I love you either."

Alex doesn't speak. He begins walking again. We are at the top of the stairs. At the door to my room. "We cannot get married, Alex."

"We have to." He looks at me, and sadness fills his eyes.

"Why? You are free here, right?"

"We are free to do what the king says." Alex lowers his voice. "But I thought you would be happier about it."

I am not sure how to respond. I am happy, part of me. But another part is unhappy. That part feels distant, like the memory. But it is there. "I'm confused."

Alex closes his eyes. When he opens them, a different look emerges in his eyes. Determined. Almost angry. "You should get to sleep." He opens the door for me and walks off. I watch him go. He does not stop at his room. He continues down the hall.

Something in me warns that none of this is right. But I don't know why or what. One thing I do know is that Alex knows more than he is telling me. I wait until he begins walking up the stairs that lead to his father's suite, and as quietly as I can, I follow him.

CHAPTER TWENTY-NINE

don't like it."

I am crouching behind the door to the king's room. I can see through the thin slat that separates the door from the wall. I try not to move or breathe.

"She is a lovely girl," the king says. "She is directly from the State. We have learned much from her already, have we not? And the people seem to love her. They will cry tears of joy at your wedding."

"She doesn't even understand marriage, Father." Alex runs a hand through his blond hair. "The Scientists there make children in labs."

"It doesn't matter what she thinks or what she knows."

"Couldn't we wait?" Alex groans. "It's only been a few days. This is all happening so fast. I don't want to force her into this."

"You are the prince." The king raises his voice, but he remains reclined on his bed. "And she is not forced. You saw her tonight. She is happy. And why shouldn't she be? She will one day be queen of Athens."

"She wasn't happy because of that, and you know it."

The king locks his hands behind his head. "It is a kindness, Alex. She is new and frightened, so much to process. We are giving her the best of what we have to offer in order to make her adjustment smooth."

"But drugging her, Father?" I put a hand to my mouth to keep from shouting out. "She feels happy because we are *making* her feel happy. But I have been with her. I have seen when the effects wear off. It isn't fair to her."

My feelings have been the result of drugs? What does he mean when the effects wear off? Am I drugged now? Of course I am drugged now. I just accepted a marriage proposal. To a virtual stranger who does not love me and who I do not love.

I think back on the week I have been here. I recall being happy at seeing Alex, his eyes, his attentions. But I barely remember anything before my arrival. It is blurry, like a picture hidden underneath water. These feelings are manufactured, my memories repressed. What kind of place is this? What kind of men are these? Alex's shout brings me back.

"I won't do this." Alex's hands are shaking. "I know I said I would, but that was before . . ."

"I believe you do have feelings for your fiancée." The king smiles, but anger appears in his eyes. "How nice."

"She is a human being. We should not test on her. We should not force her into marriage so soon."

The king stands, towering over his son, his smile evaporated. "She is a subject of Athens. My subject. As are you. You would do well to remember that. Someday you will be king; you will make the decisions. But for now, I am ruler. I am the authority. I make the rules. If I want to test our pharmaceuticals on our subjects, then I will. If I want my son to marry a refugee from the State, he will. Do you understand?"

Alex looks down, his face red, fists clenched. "Yes, sir."

"Very well." The king sits again. The silence stretches out for so long, I am sure the conversation is over. I begin to silently retreat back to my chamber, but the king's voice breaks through, deep and almost too quiet for me to hear him. "You will be happy to know I have changed my mind about your sister."

I look back through the space behind the door. Alex's face lightens. "You won't use her for . . . ?"

"No, I won't." The king stretches out on his bed, pauses for several moments before he speaks. "We can save her, thanks to your fiancée."

"Thalli?" Alex's voice cracks. "You're going to use Thalli?"

"Why not?" The king shrugs. "It's obvious the State won't send anyone after her. They wanted her dead. My hope when I heard of her arrival was that there would be more, that we could finally get our hands on what they have, the way my father always dreamed. But that won't happen. She came alone, with nothing but that transport of hers and a suit we don't need. And truly, son, I think we've exceeded the State in technology. From what Thalli told us, there is nothing they have that we want. They don't even produce weapons. They dig into people's brains and repress their emotions with their science. We can do the same with our drugs. They limit the population; so do we. But they live underground, afraid of what's on the surface. We are looking to expand our horizons, take over the earth. So let them have their little world. We don't need it. And we don't need her. But no one here needs to know that. They need to love her and cheer for her and be happy she's marrying the heir to the Athenian throne. We will do all we can to ensure Thalli is deeply loved by all."

The king smiles, and the sight of it makes my stomach want to rid itself of every decadent food I consumed. "Then when New Hope takes her and violently murders her, the Athenians will gladly go to war. I won't have to argue with them or deal with these ridiculous guilty consciences. They will finally and completely destroy those people and claim the land that should have been ours from the start."

I am sick. I don't even know if I can move from this spot. What have I done? What have they done? I am being drugged. I will be killed? And for what? So the innocent people in New Hope can be eradicated to satiate this man's greed? I came to help promote peace. But I will start a war. A war meant to kill everyone I love.

CHAPTER THIRTY

A lex rushes from his father's room. I will wait here until the king's breathing is regular enough to assure me he is asleep.

The reality of this situation makes my head hurt. The attraction I have been feeling for Alex is manufactured. I assume the drug is administered through the food. Or the perfume. Of course it's the perfume, "made especially for me," the woman said. Made from the pharmaceuticals they specialize in. It makes me forget why I am here, who I am, what I know. I am just relieved it hasn't made me so unaware that I told them about my relationship with New Hope. So far, my friends are safe. But not for long. When will the king kill me? How much time do I have?

I need to escape. In our travels I have noted there is only one exit from Athens, and that is guarded by several men, who are large and carry weapons designed to prevent people from leaving. Peter scaled a wall from the roof of one of the factories. He explained how to do that, but he also warned that I had to be alone when I did it. But the guards are always nearby. There will be even more now that I am Alex's fiancée.

Bile rises into my throat as fear paralyzes me. *"Though I walk through the valley of the shadow of death, I will fear no evil."* The thought calms me, reminds me of my talk with John, of the Designer who cares for me. He allowed me to survive the State, to arrive safely in New Hope. He is with me. That is what the psalm says. I take a deep breath. I need him to show me what to do. How to avoid the drugs, how to get a message to my friends, how to escape.

The king is snoring. I lean my head out the door and see a guard walking from one end of the hallway to the other. One end has stairs that lead to my room. The other has stairs that lead to the workers' quarters. I do not want to go there. Someone might be awake and see me. I cannot be seen leaving here. I need to get to the stairs that lead back down to my bedroom. I pray that the Designer will make me invisible.

When the guard passes the door and walks toward the other end of the hallway, I move as quickly and as quietly as I can. I am almost halfway down the stairs when I trip over the dress and fall hard down two steps. I bite back a groan, but it is too late. The guard heard me. I hear his heavy feet moving toward me. I run down the hallway.

Right into Alex.

"Who is down here?"

Alex pulls me to him, smothering my face in his chest. He leans into me, his mouth at my ear. "Don't say anything." He then jerks his head up in the direction of the guard. I keep my head hidden. Alex's heart is beating as fast as mine is.

"Sorry, Reginald." Alex's voice is quiet, calm. He even injects a bit of nervous laughter. "I was just spending some time with my fiancée. You know . . ."

"Oh, I know." The guard laughs, and I want to pull away and tell him what is really going on. But then, Alex very likely just saved my life. I keep my head down and feel the guard give Alex a pat on the back. "Sorry to disturb you, Your Majesty."

Alex doesn't let go until the guard is down the stairs. When he pulls away, he puts a finger to his mouth and motions me to follow him to his room.

I shake my head. Alex lifts his hands in the gesture of surrender, mouths *Please*. His eyes dart back to the stairs.

I go, but I keep my back to the door after Alex closes it. He defended me back there, but he also stood by and allowed me to be drugged all this time. I cannot trust him.

"I went to your room after I left my father's chambers," Alex whispers. He takes a step closer, his eyes full of sympathy, kindness. But maybe the drugs make me think that. I cannot even trust my own thoughts anymore. "You followed me."

He isn't asking a question. He knows. Of course he knows. He heard me on the stairs. But he did not tell the guard. "Why did you lie for me?"

"You were hiding in the king's quarters." Alex runs a hand

through his hair. "Do you have any idea what would happen to you if he found out?"

"I don't know. I would be killed violently and the murder blamed on New Hope?"

Alex closes his eyes. When he opens them, he points to a sitting area at the far side of the room. Away from the door. "Please sit and let me explain."

I refuse to move. My hand is on the doorknob. "I heard it all. Your father tells everyone what to do and they do it. If he is feeling generous, he drugs them so they think they want to do what he has commanded. But if not, they just deal with it. Because he is the king. And you are next in line for the throne."

"I am not like my father." Alex is standing inches from me now. His voice is still low but firm. His blue eyes are huge in the dark room. He seems genuine. "Please, just listen to me."

I recall his conversation with the king. Alex was not happy with the plan. He tried to defend me. He obviously tried to defend his sister in the past. The drugging was not his idea, nor was the marriage or the murder. The least I can do is listen to what he has to say. "Fine. Explain."

I walk to a chair covered in—what else?—black. Alex sits across from me, hands on his knees. "How much did you hear?"

I tell him what I heard. If I am to have any possible ally here, it will be Alex. And if he turns out to be another enemy— what does it matter? The ruler of the country is plotting my murder. I need someone more powerful than him to save me. Thankfully, I know someone like that. I breathe a prayer to him, asking him to keep the anger from me, to help me think the best of this boy—my "fiancé."

"Is there more?" I ask, after I relayed the conversation I overheard.

"No." Alex reaches for my hand. I do not allow him to take it. "Father has been seeking war with New Hope for years, and we've had some successful skirmishes. But the soldiers are uncomfortable taking the whole village."

"What about you?" I hold my breath waiting for the answer.

"The people of New Hope have done some cruel things to us in the past."

"How do you know?"

"My father—"

"And he is always truthful?" I twist my lips.

"He wanted to have my sister killed in order to start a war." Alex looks away from me, his Adam's apple bobbing. "I would not have let that happen. I was trying to find another way."

"And then I came along."

"I won't let him use you either." Alex looks at me now, his gaze so intense my mouth goes dry. "We do not need to win a war that way."

"You're opposed to killing innocent people?" I think of the villagers.

"Yes."

"What about the people of New Hope?"

"We don't have time to talk about that now. We have to get you out of here." Alex rubs his temples.

"But the only place to go is New Hope." I raise my eyebrows as he meets my gaze.

Alex shakes his head. "They are our enemies."

I debate whether or not to reveal to him the extent of my lies. I was angry at Alex for keeping this from me. What will he do when he finds out what I've kept from him? Will he refuse to help? Decide I am worthy of this punishment? I close my eyes to pray.

John once told me the truth will set me free. I pray he is right.

CHAPTER THIRTY-ONE

You're a spy."

Alex is upset. I understand why. I thought the truth would set me free. And I do feel better for having told it. But Alex certainly does not look free.

"How do I even know if I can believe this?" Alex paces back and forth. "You say the people of New Hope want peace. But what if that's a lie too? Your plan all along may have been to lure me out, and this is the perfect way. Then I die, and New Hope comes and attacks Athens."

I groan. This is so complicated. Why did I think it would be simple? "They wouldn't do that."

"How do you know? You believe them?"

"Yes." I raise my hands in surrender. "They are good people. Kind."

"But you thought that about us too, right?" Alex stops and lifts his eyebrows.

"You drugged me." I think of how I had been feeling about this town, about Alex. Shame battles with anger.

"I didn't drug you."

"But your father did—the king." I lower my voice, afraid the guard might walk by and overhear us. "The leaders of New Hope at least helped me. Some of them doubted us and were wary of us, but I'd take that over being controlled!"

"Why are you so sure they were helping you?" Alex folds his arms across his chest. "How do you know they weren't using you too?"

"They didn't ask me to come." I step closer to Alex. He will not convince me the villagers of New Hope are evil. "I volunteered, insisted."

"For what reason?"

"They want peace." I look Alex in the eyes, will him to listen to me. "The Athenians take what is theirs. Some of the men burned down a house—with people inside. They live in fear of you."

"As they should." Alex's eyes harden. But I understand what he is doing. The same thing I did for years: he is repeating what he has been taught.

"In the State, we were taught that the Scientists worked for our good." I sit on Alex's couch. He remains standing but he is listening. "The rules, the programming, separating us in pods, eliminating—*attempting* to eliminate—emotions and free thought: all of that was to help us be better people than the generations that went before us. And it made sense. I believed them. I still do believe they think they are doing what's best. But I disagree with them. I don't think it's right."

"Of course it isn't." Alex plants his hands on his hips.

"Neither is ruling by force." I say this softly, but it still sounds harsh. I pause as Alex considers this. "Taking what doesn't belong to you? Planning a murder to incite war? That isn't right."

Alex sighs and sits beside me on the couch. "You know I won't allow that. But my father is following principles that have been in place for millennia. People need a strong ruler. They *should* fear him. Pure democracy places decisions in the hands of people who have no business making decisions."

"So harming innocent people . . . that's the sign of a good ruler?"

Alex leans his head back. "It's complicated."

"Drugging people so you get what you want without argument is a sign of a good ruler?"

"Thalli, what do you expect me to do?" Alex's gaze drills into mine. "He is my father and the king. We have laws."

"So did the State." I stare right back at Alex.

"But their laws were ridiculous."

"Their laws condemned me to death." I look toward the door. "Yours have done the same."

Neither of us speaks for several moments. "So you think New Hope is perfect, then? They should rule over us?"

I think of the chaos after Diana arrived. How some of the people wanted to send her back, knowing that would mean her death. People were so angry, hurt, scared. "No, they aren't perfect. But they don't deserve to be destroyed."

"What do you want me to do?" Alex stands. "I can try to help you escape, but that won't solve the problem."

"It will make it worse." I stand to join Alex. "Your father will argue that New Hope offered me refuge, and he will send an army out after me. He'll do even more damage to that village."

"So what, then?"

The answer comes to me quickly. "Escape with me."

Alex takes in a sharp breath. "What?"

"If you come with me, your father won't attack. He won't risk losing you. You are heir to the throne."

"You don't know my father." Alex's jaw flexes with an emotion I cannot identify.

"It will allow us to go back to New Hope." The plan is coming together even as I speak. "You can get to know the people, talk with them. Make a plan for peace. Then you can return to your father. Help him to see the benefits of working together."

"You think more of my father than you should." Alex shakes his head. "It will not be that simple."

"Do you have another plan?"

Alex sighs. "No."

"Then we escape."

"No." Alex walks toward me. "We will not escape. We will walk out with his blessing."

"What?" I see a plan forming in Alex's eyes. "How?"

Alex places his hands on my shoulders. "After we get married."

CHAPTER THIRTY-TWO

am getting married.

This does not feel right. Not in any way. I think of John's story. He married Amy after they had known each other for a long time. They had fallen in love. They chose each other and were married before the Designer, promising to stay together until one of them died. But even now, decades after Amy died, John still thinks of her, misses her.

I do not love Alex. I thought I loved Berk. But I threw that love away when I left. For his own good. I don't even know if we were right for each other. I am doubting that love the longer I am away from him. But is that a result of the medicines I have been inhaling, or is it truly what is in my heart? I can't trust my own emotions anymore.

I can't deny that I have some feelings for Alex. He is certainly attractive. He is kind. We have been thrown together in an impossible situation. The thought of marrying him isn't repulsive.

Anyway, Alex is right—we have no other choice but to marry. I recall John saying marriage is difficult, no matter who you are with, that it takes work and you don't always feel love, but you stick with that person anyway. *"Till death do you part."*

When we marry, Alex will tell his father we are going away for a few days. It is tradition. A "honeymoon." The king has a special home outside the walls of Athens. Part of the university that used to be there. No one ever goes there because there is nothing around it—no food, no factories. Somehow, this one residence survived when everything around it fell. The first king of Athens claimed it as his right, but it is only used for private meetings. And the days following a royal wedding.

But we will not actually go to this residence. For that, I am glad. If this were a real marriage and a real honeymoon, what would we do all those days alone together? There are questions I am afraid to ask. I have an idea, but I have no one to ask whether or not my idea is right. Whatever it is that happens then will not happen with us because we will go in the opposite direction. We will go to New Hope. We will tell the people there we want to negotiate peace. Our marriage will provide proof of that.

I am sure the king will not harm the village of New Hope if it means harming Alex as well. But Alex can get to know the people. He can report back to the king that they are kind, hardworking people who simply want to live the way they have lived for the past forty years. We can establish trade between the two cities. Peace. I pray that Gerald and his band will accept that peace, that they won't harm Alex before they can get to know him. I don't want to lead Alex into an ambush.

"Thalli?" Helen stands outside my door, as if she is afraid to come in.

We have spoken very little, but since the announcement of Alex's and my engagement, she has smiled at me in passing. I hoped we would be able to talk more. I cannot see her without thinking of Peter. I wish the wedding could be theirs and not ours. I am sure they would understand what to do on a honeymoon.

"Helen." She is so different than her brother. Not at all self-assured. She seems frightened. And sad. So sad. Even now that she knows she will not have to be killed. "Come and sit."

"I should have come to you earlier." Her voice is quiet, like a piano key that is barely touched. I have to lean close to hear her. "I apologize."

"There hasn't been much time." I want to help her relax. She seems so tense. "I arrived, toured the city, got engaged . . ."

Helen looks at me. Her eyes are as dark as her brother's are light. I can barely see her pupils. But her eyelashes are long like Alex's, and her hair is just a shade darker blond than his. She is beautiful. "My father's decisions are rash."

There is more to that statement than just the words she has said. There is an anger behind them. Helen looks out the window. I remain quiet, let her think.

"My brother believes you can be trusted." As she says that, I see some of the fear beginning to release its hold on her.

"I want very much to help." I am not sure if Alex told his

sister of our plan. I do not want to say anything in case he hasn't. Helen is older than I, but I still have a desire to protect her.

"There are things you don't understand." Helen's gaze darts toward the door. She stands, looks out of it, then shuts it firmly behind her. "Alex told you our mother died?"

"Yes."

Helen walks quietly back to the couch. She changes subjects so quickly. I wish I could see inside her brain to know how all this connects.

"Did he tell you how she died?"

"No."

Helen takes a deep breath. "She was murdered."

"Murdered?" I cannot imagine how that was even possible. This palace is so well guarded. "Who would kill the queen?"

"My father."

I gasp. The king murdered his own wife? Surely that isn't right.

"You deserve to know this." Helen looks at me, her eyes full of compassion. "Alex agrees. You should know what you are facing—*who* you are facing."

"Why didn't Alex tell me?"

"Because my brother wants to protect me." Helen looks down. She is silent.

I want to shake her, force the story out of her. But I wait because I know I need to.

"I am not the king's daughter."

"What?"

"Before my mother was given in marriage to my father, she was in love with another man." Helen takes in a ragged breath.

171

"But her parents forced her to end that relationship. The king saw my mother, and he wanted her for his son. No one refuses the king. It is an honor to marry the prince."

"So I've heard," I say. Helen lets out a slight smile and gazes at the floor.

"She married him. But she did not love him. He was not kind." Helen looks up sharply. "Alex is not like him. He has tried, in order to please him, to behave the way the king wants him to behave. But Alex is a good man. He will be a good husband."

Husband. The sound of that makes my stomach hurt. "I know."

"Our mother could not forget her first love. They met secretly. The king—prince at the time—was so busy with his training, he didn't notice her absences. When she became pregnant, the prince assumed the child was his. When his father died and he ascended the throne, he had little time for my mother or for Alex and me. My mother was sure he would never find out. Besides, for several years my mother wasn't even sure who the father was. It could have been the king."

The ancient way of procreation is still confusing to me. How could she not know who the father was? "How did your mother know whose you were?"

"It was my eyes." Helen looks at me, and I am again struck by how dark they are. "No one on either my mother's or the king's side has eyes this color. My mother thought little of that, but when I was six, one of the men of the city approached her. He studied science. He told her it was biologically impossible for her and my father to have a child with eyes my color. He knew of my mother's relationship with my biological father before her marriage."

"He guessed the truth."

"Yes." Helen closes her eyes. "And he made her pay him to remain quiet about it."

"How awful."

Helen nods. "For years she gave him whatever he asked for. But five years ago, he was arrested. One of the guards saw him with one of the palace treasures. He refused to say anything. He wouldn't speak to the officers of the law. He insisted on having a private audience with the king."

"He told the king about your father."

Helen's eyes fill with tears. "The king was so angry. He ordered my mother's death, my father's death, and the death of the man who told him."

"How could he do that?" To kill his own wife—and two others—because he was angry? This is far worse than the Scientists. At least they believed they were helping the State when they chose to annihilate others.

"He is king." Helen says this so softly, I can barely hear it. "His father taught him the king can do anything, with no consequences. He also taught him that anyone who undermines the king's authority must be killed."

"But his own wife?" I am sick. "The people allow him to do that?"

"The people did not know." Helen wipes a tear from her cheek. "My mother didn't even know it was happening until it was too late. The king had my father and the other man taken outside the city with some of the guards. They told the people they had been killed in a run-in with the people from New Hope. But Mother . . . at first, he just kept her isolated. We didn't understand why. Alex and I weren't allowed to see her.

Then we were told she was very sick. Doctors came in and out of her room.

"The whole city was worried about her. She was beloved. Our mother was everything Father was not: kind, generous, concerned about the welfare of others. Father knew her death could not come suddenly. Even though he believes in the sovereignty of the king, he recognizes that if the people are too unhappy, they could rebel. That would create more problems for him."

"He poisoned her?"

"We specialize in pharmaceuticals." Helen shrugs. "He worked with one of the developers. The developer was killed not long after Mother died."

I want to ask her to stop. This is too horrible. Unspeakable. No wonder Helen is so sad.

"Alex and I snuck into her room one night when Father was out on a raid. She knew she was dying. She wanted us to know the truth. About everything. She was so sick. I think she was just holding on until she could see us." Helen pauses, too emotional to continue. "She died the next day."

"What did you do?"

"Nothing." Helen uses her fingertips to wipe the tears from her eyes. "What *could* we do? I was fifteen; Alex was thirteen. We were so scared of the king. But at least we were allowed to grieve. And the whole city grieved with us. She had a beautiful funeral."

"I am so sorry."

Helen looks at me, her expression serious. "This is the family you are marrying into, Thalli. The king killed his own wife; he was willing to kill me. He is planning to kill you. And he won't stop unless someone stops him. Alex and I agree on most things, but on this we are divided: The king will not be persuaded into any kind of peace with New Hope. He wants to conquer it. And he will stop at nothing—nothing—in order to accomplish that goal."

CHAPTER THIRTY-THREE

am standing on the most ornate transport I have ever seen. Alex called it a chariot. It is gold with huge wheels supporting a platform that is open in the back and closed in the front. A massive black horse is in front of it, with two golden ropes going from the back of the horse to my hands. I am nervous about being in control of such a large animal. I worry that he will run so fast I will topple over, the chariot crushing me.

But even that thought is more pleasant than thinking of the reason I am in this transport. It is my wedding day. The day I marry a boy I do not love to trick a king whom I fear. So much could go wrong. If Helen is right, we have to convince those in Athens to rise up against the king. If Alex is right, the king might be willing to listen to reason if it is couched in the right terms. But either way, we have only seven days to earn the people's trust and come up with a plan. The feast held in our honor will begin here in Athens seven days after our wedding. Seven days from today.

I have avoided thinking of the wedding. It has not been difficult, considering all the other circumstances I have been forced to consider. But standing here, wearing the gown Alex's mother wore, surrounded by palace guards, the reality of this suddenly comes into clear view.

I am going to be married. In a matter of hours. And John says that marriage is a promise to the Designer and it is to last until one of us dies. Weeks ago, I had imagined that if I ever got married, it would be to Berk. And it would be years from now. After we had settled in New Hope, established our lives there. I had dreams of teaching music to children. Learning more from John about the Designer. Never did I have dreams of becoming the princess of a city where the ruler is a tyrannical murderer.

"It is time." The guard beside me motions for me to slap the ropes against the horse to begin the procession.

I almost fall as the horse moves forward, taking my arms with him. I relax my arms and bend my elbows as Alex advised me. It is hard to do. The horse is so strong. But we eventually find a rhythm. I keep one foot planted in front of the other so I don't lean forward.

"Smile at the subjects." Another guard motions toward the people.

This is an exciting day for them. A royal wedding does not happen often. I have been reminded of that several times this week. *"Smile at the people. Nod. Accept their praise. Keep your elbows bent."*

Sometimes I think this is a dream—induced, perhaps, by the drugs Athens is famous for. It seems even less real than the simulations I was placed under at the State with the Scientists. I want to feel the back of my head to see if a hole is there, the way I tested to see if I was under their control. But I cannot spare either hand.

I wish this were a dream. The closer this chariot takes me to the palace, the less I want to go. I am not as brave as I thought. And I am not nearly as selfless as I pretend to be.

I have hardly seen Alex the last few days. I have gone through "beauty treatments" that seem much more like torture than treatment. All sorts of oils and vegetation have been placed on all parts of my body. My hair has been curled, straightened, and curled again. Hundreds of pins hold it in a beautiful style that, combined with all the pencils and powders layered on my face, makes me look less like myself than I have ever been.

They all tell me this is part of the royal treatment so I will be beautiful on my wedding day. But beauty is not worth all of this pain. Whatever I was before is just fine with me. Will Alex even recognize me under this façade?

I look around after being prodded once again by one of the guards. People are shouting, crying, throwing flowers. Alex says this wedding tradition dates back to the ancient Athens his grandfather was so enamored with. This isn't like the wedding John spoke of. We are not in a church. I am not in white. And the Designer has not even been mentioned.

I think of the words John showed me, about a table being

prepared in the presence of my enemies. Is this what that meant? But these people—smiling, crying, waving—they are not my enemies. Alex and Helen are certainly not enemies. It is just the king—their ruler. What would this city be like if he was removed from power? I look around at his guards. They will do whatever he says. Even kill people. Removing him from power will be impossible. He is far too protected. I close my eyes for a moment. Surely, the Designer has a plan.

"Greet your people." The guard interrupts my prayer.

We reach the palace. Guards line each side of the entrance. Their swords are held above their heads to create a type of arch. It is an uncomfortable feeling, riding beneath these swords. What if the king instructed one of them to drop a sword on me? He could say that guard was a spy from New Hope, begin the war that way. I hold my breath until that danger is past. But the thought is there. What is to stop the king from killing me today? And what better time than now, when all the people are gathered to see it?

"*Even though I walk through the valley of the shadow of death, I will fear no evil.*" I feel the Designer with me, beside me. I will not fear.

The chariot stops. Alex is below me, dressed in purple from head to toe. He looks very handsome with his golden hair curling just above his shoulders and his smile directed at me. I am suddenly thankful that the king has a son my age, not twenty years older. I am sure I would not be feeling nearly so willing were that the case. He holds out his hand. He is smiling, but fear flickers in his eyes. I hand the ropes to a guard and step down, careful not to trip over the long skirt.

Music plays, but it is recorded music. It sounds stale. I

imagined majestic sounds—brass and strings together. But this music matches the ceremony: forced, unnatural, fake.

Alex and I walk together toward the king. He is in full regalia: robes, a crown, even a scepter. If it were not so formal and frightening, I would laugh at the arrogance of it all.

"You look beautiful," Alex whispers into my ear, his hand caressing my arm.

I need to remember that this is my wedding day. It might not be what—or when—I imagined. But I need to enjoy it. I will not get another.

"You look very handsome yourself." I smile at my soon-to-be husband, meaning it.

The king opens his mouth to speak, but no sound comes out. Instead, we hear the sound of shouting from behind us. One voice in particular stands out from the others.

"Stop this now."

Berk.

He is here.

CHAPTER THIRTY-FOUR

et her go." Berk stares down the guards with all the swords.
Myriad emotions battle for space in my mind and
heart. Anger seems to be winning. I have a plan. Alex and I
have a plan. Berk has ruined it. He will reveal the truth of who I
am. He will ruin the chances that we had to come to New Hope
and negotiate peace. Once again, Berk has assumed the role of
rescuer. But I do not need his rescuing.

"Who are you?" The king steps forward, between Alex and
me.

"My name is Berk." His voice is strong, angry. I have never
heard him like this. "I escaped the State to find refuge in New
Hope—"

"Then you are an enemy."

"I came alone," Berk says. "Unarmed. I came only for Thalli."

I try to look past the throng of people. I was sure he came with others. But the voices I heard were not those of the men of New Hope. They were Athenians protesting. Berk is alone. He walked into Athens alone.

"You have interrupted a royal wedding, Berk." The king waves his hand and the crowd parts. I see Berk now. His shoulders are slumped—he is exhausted. But he holds his head high.

"The bride cannot desire this wedding." Berk steps forward and the king tenses beside me.

"To marry the future king of Athens is a great honor."

"To be forced into any marriage is dishonorable."

The crowd gasps. The king slams his scepter on the ground. Berk is close enough for me to see his eyes. They are on me. Gentle, concerned, questioning.

"Guards." The king barely contains his anger. "Arrest this man."

"No." I grab the king's sleeve, almost falling to my knees in the process. He will kill Berk. He will kill him and think nothing of it. I cannot allow that to happen. "Please. He means no harm."

"He means no harm?" The king's voice is so loud in my ear that I feel its vibrations deep in my skull. "He dares to enter *my* city uninvited, interrupt *my* son's wedding, make demands of *me*?"

"He does not know the laws of this city." I dare to look into the king's face. It is red, his eyes bloodshot. "He only means to help."

"We will deal with him later." The king motions to the guards. "*After* the wedding."

"No."

I look at Berk. He has not spoken. His mouth is a thin line as the guards yank his hands behind his back.

"Father." It is Alex. He is speaking low, moving closer to the king. "The moment has been sullied. I do not want this memory of my wedding day. Please allow us to postpone the festivities."

Berk looks at me. He is asking me with his eyes if I am safe. I smile and nod, wanting him to know I have not been harmed, that I am concerned for him, not for me. I try not to think of what his appearance means to our plans. I try not to think that his appearance may mean we will both die. I cannot think that. The king is whispering to Alex. I catch only a few words of their exchange. Those words, though, give me hope.

"Ladies and gentlemen." The king's voice is still loud, but it has changed in tone. No longer short, staccato, and angry; it is warm, legato. I still hear the anger underneath, but the people seem oblivious to it. "I apologize for this unwelcome interruption to this most special of days. My son has requested that his wedding be postponed. He wants to look back on his wedding day with nothing but fond memories of his people rejoicing and his bride glowing with love."

Berk pulls away from the guards, but he is pulled back by his hair. His eyes close and he steps back once again. I cannot move.

"Therefore I have decreed that the festivities begun today will resume tomorrow." The king motions to the crowd. "Enjoy today with your own families and return tomorrow at this same time to watch your prince marry."

The people clap—a slow, tentative clap at first, turning into boisterous applause with shouts and whistles. Are the people drugged here to obey this king the way I was drugged earlier? How is it that so many people would so blindly follow this man unless they were drugged? Then I think of the State. We blindly followed the Scientists. But we were designed to do that. It was part of our makeup. Or was it? Perhaps it was simply conditioning. Like these people. If all a people ever know is blind obedience, perhaps this is the only response they are capable of giving. And perhaps just like in the State, anomalies are here too. Those who secretly refuse to obey.

"Take the prisoner to the holding chamber. I will deal with him personally."

I want to run and throw myself between the guards and Berk, but I do not. If I do, I will lose any chance of being able to save him. So I stand and watch him be taken away, my chest heaving with unshed tears.

I will fear no evil. I will fear no evil. I repeat those words over and over, wanting them to be true. But I am failing. I am afraid, so very afraid. Deliverance seems impossible. Did the person who wrote those words ever experience anything like this? I wish John were here to tell me, to help me. But he is not here.

I have never felt so alone.

CHAPTER THIRTY-FIVE

Please let me see him." I am in Alex's room now, begging him to take me to Berk. "I can't let your father kill him. I can't."

Alex walks over to me, his eyes full of compassion. He places his hands on my shoulders and forces me to look in his eyes. "We can do nothing right now. But be assured—my father will not kill him."

"How can you know?"

Alex removes his hands and looks at the ground.

"How, Alex?" It is my turn to force his gaze to mine. "How can you know that?"

Alex takes a deep breath. "He does not kill in secret."

"What?"

"Punishment is very public here. Everyone must watch."

"But your mother and Diana's father?" They were not killed publicly.

"Father did not want their crimes discovered." Alex moves to his couch and sits. "It would have been an embarrassment to him. But when his power is challenged—he goes to great lengths to ensure the people understand that will not be tolerated."

I recall what Peter said about his parents—burned to death. I shudder at the thought. "What will he do to Berk?"

"We'll think of something." Alex looks at me again, pain in his eyes. "I promise."

"Tell me the worst that could happen."

"No, Thalli." Alex rubs his face with his hands.

"I need to know the worst that could happen."

"Why?"

I pause. "Because…I'd rather be prepared than be surprised."

A small smile appears. "You'd make a good ruler."

I will not allow him to change the direction of our conversation. "Tell me." I move to sit next to Alex so I can hear the next words clearly.

"Father prefers torture. It isn't enough to simply kill an enemy. He believes the people must be educated. They must know that disobedience comes at a high cost."

"I thought perhaps they were drugged and that was why they were so compliant."

"No, not drugged," Alex says. "Not often, anyway. Fear is a far greater and longer-lasting method of maintaining control."

"What kind of torture?"

"Please, Thalli." Alex looks away. "There are some images that will never be erased from my mind. I don't want you to be forced to imagine them."

I want to press him, but he is right. He is trying to protect me. "How much time then?"

Alex pauses. "I don't know. Sometimes Father makes the prisoners wait, starves them, makes them beg for death. Other times he wants them to come fighting."

"How often does this happen?"

"Not often," Alex says. "Once every five or six years, I suppose. People try to rebel. He finds their leader and . . ."

"What do you think he will do with Berk?"

I can see him debating within himself what to say. "He wants the wedding to take place soon. When he has a plan in place, he doesn't want that plan thwarted in any way."

"So he will try to kill Berk soon?"

Alex looks at me. "I will not let him."

"Can I see Berk?"

"Absolutely not. You must appear to be complying with the king's wishes."

"Or he will kill me too?" I fold my arms across my chest. "He's already planning that anyway."

"He will drug you again." Alex raises his eyebrows at me. "I have convinced him you do not need the drugs. But if he feels you are being too troublesome, he will insist."

I think of how I felt under the influence of those pharmaceuticals. My mind was foggy, my emotions changed. I do not want that. "All right. But I have to do something. Please."

"Act like everything is fine, like you want to get married. Try to win my father's affections. That will make it harder for him to have you killed. I am trying to convince him you are more valuable alive than dead."

"Try to win his affections?" I think I might rather die. This barbaric tyrant who is willing to kill his own wife, to torture Berk? Pretend that none of that matters? I do not think I am capable of that.

"He is not all bad."

I forget this is Alex's father. I do not even know what that would be like, to have parents who raised you, whom you love. Our Monitors were the closest things to parents we had, but they rotated out every few months. We never bonded with them. Never bonded with anyone but those in our pod.

"He truly believes this is the right way to rule people. He wants to be feared, it is true, but he is convinced that fear is the only way to reach our goals for this city."

"And killing people? This helps reach your goals?"

"They aren't my goals." Alex releases a heavy sigh. "But I fear Father too. I don't think he would kill me. He has no other heir. But I am not foolish enough to believe I could oppose him without facing any consequences."

Why did I ever think that peace between Athens and New Hope would come easily? I am beginning to wonder if it will come at all. And I am convinced it will never come as long as the king lives. But I cannot say that to Alex. As much as he fears his father and realizes his practices are wrong, I doubt Alex could ever bring himself to hurt his father.

So, then, is it up to me? Can I kill this king to save his people? To save New Hope? To save Berk? Can I justify murder? What would John say? What about the Designer? Would he condone this?

I stand up to leave Alex's room. I cannot tell him what I am thinking. I cannot even allow him to guess. "I will do what you ask."

But that is not all I will do.

CHAPTER THIRTY-SIX

'll take you to see Berk." Helen snuck into my room just minutes after Alex left. She brought a guard's uniform and hat.

"No one will ever believe I am a man." I am thin and short. I do not have much of a chest, but enough is sticking out to make people look twice.

"People believe whatever makes sense. It makes sense for me to be escorted through the palace with a guard. No one will think anything of it."

"But why are you escorted? Alex isn't."

"Alex doesn't want to escape." Helen's voice sounds heavy, as if it is weighted down.

"But you do."

Helen lets out a loud exhale.

"Because you fear for your life?"

Helen looks at me. "You care for Berk?"

I do not understand this change in the conversation. Perhaps she told me all she wants to tell me about her life and her difficulties. "Very much."

"I cared for someone too." A tear rolls down her cheek. "He escaped."

I do not speak. Although I know what she is about to say, I also know she needs to say it. Freedom is found in speaking the truth.

Helen takes a deep breath. "Please don't tell anyone I am telling you this. Not even Alex."

"Alex doesn't know?" That surprises me. I was sure the siblings told each other everything.

"Alex didn't approve." Helen shrugs. "Not of Peter and certainly not of my desire to escape."

"Peter?" I try to keep my voice even, but she must hear something in my voice that betrays me.

Helen gasps. "You know him?"

"I saw him."

"You saw him?"

I tell Helen the whole truth—about landing in New Hope, staying there, getting to know the people, coming here to try to find a way to bring peace to the cities. Helen, though, hears only Peter's name.

"So he is alive . . ." A light enters her eyes—hope.

"He was injured. In a fire. But the last I saw of him, he appeared to be almost fully recovered. His sister was with him."

"Diana made it?" Helen closes her eyes as a tear slips down her cheek. "My father told me Peter was killed." Helen puts a hand to her mouth to stifle a sob. "But I knew he was alive. I knew it. Thank you."

"But how were you able to know him?" This was a question I was never able to ask Peter. Carey and Kristie told me Peter and his family were ostracized from the royal family because of their refusal to do what the king asked.

"I was given more freedom before," Helen says, a tiny smile on her lips. "Especially after my mother died. Father—the king—didn't care where I went or what I did. And I wanted nothing more than to be far away from here. Everywhere I went reminded me of my mother. It was so painful."

I wait as Helen wipes tears from her eyes with the tips of her fingers. She is so well mannered. Even when she's upset.

"One day I just walked as far as I could go. I ended up at a stable where Peter was caring for his horses. We just started talking. I didn't tell him who I was. He had lived on the outskirts for so long, he had no idea I was royalty. He was the first friend I ever had who just knew me as Helen. Not 'the princess.' Other than Alex and our mother, Peter was the only person who ever treated me with kindness and never wanted anything in return."

"But Alex didn't approve?"

"Alex thinks like a king," Helen says. "Not regarding the treatment of others. My brother would never do to people what Father does. But he does believe in the purity of our line. And he never considered marriage for love. We were taught, from the time we were small, that the lower classes could marry for love. But royals do not. It is beneath us."

I understand. Until recently, I was not taught about marriage at all. It is still a strange concept. Mysterious.

"But the more time I spent with Peter, the more I knew I could never marry anyone else."

"What happened?"

"Father discovered us."

"How?"

"He has spies everywhere." Helen's onyx eyes glisten. "And he had Peter's family watched because of their 'rebelliousness.' One of his spies saw us talking together, and he reported that back to Father."

"But you helped Peter escape."

"I wanted to go with him." Helen looks down at the floor, closes her eyes. "I wanted to go with him so badly. Watching him leave was the hardest thing I've ever had to do. But it would have been too much of a risk to go with him. Sometimes, though, I wish I had taken that risk. This life . . . is terrible."

"Is Alex aware that you helped Peter escape?"

Helen leans her head to the side. "I didn't tell him—I don't want him to know. He suspects. But this is something he cannot know with certainty. If he found out, Father would no doubt have me killed. And he will find out eventually. So I am waiting for the right time to escape. I was hoping to do it when you and Alex left after your wedding. But that won't happen now."

"Of course it can." I put my hand on Helen's knee. "We will not leave you behind with that man. Never."

"It won't happen because you are not marrying my brother." Helen looks me in the eyes. "You care for Berk, not Alex. And Alex deserves to marry someone who loves him, even if he doesn't see that yet."

"That's why you want to help me see Berk." Helen's sadness makes sense now. She was mourning Peter, fearing for his life.

"I don't want to just help you see him." Helen stands and leads me to the door. "I want to help you escape with him."

CHAPTER THIRTY-SEVEN

elen is right. No one even notices us. Helen plays the role of the moody daughter, shooting me angry glances as I grasp her elbow. She even winces like I am hurting her. We walk past other guards. They don't even glance up from what they're doing. We have walked down the stairs and through the grand hall. I am thankful that neither the king nor Alex has passed us. I am sure they would see through my disguise.

"Turn right before we reach the main door," Helen whispers into my ear.

I obey and find myself in a narrow corridor. "Where are we?"

"This is a secondary entrance to the cellar. We only use it during parties, to make a quick exit or entrance."

The hall ends abruptly. "Someone has sealed the exit."

Helen looks behind us, then pushes on one of the stones. The wall shifts to the side, revealing a hidden exit. "Hurry."

It is several degrees cooler inside this space than it was in the hallway. And once the door closes, it is very dark. Helen pats the wall beside us until lights flicker on—dull at first, but progressively lighter. The lights are in the ceiling, one every few feet. I cannot see the end of this passageway. "How far does this go?"

"It leads down into the cellar." Helen moves faster. "From there, we can go back up to our residential chambers or farther down to the holding chamber. My mother told me there is an exit out of the city gates somewhere here too. But she didn't know where it was."

"Have you tried to find it?"

"A few times." Helen sighs. "But I have always been caught. Guards are everywhere."

"Guards!" I stumble on one of the stones at my feet and Helen catches my arm before I fall. "How will we get past them to see Berk?"

"I have this." Helen pulls a circular object from her dress. "It's a sleeping drug. Airborne."

"How did you get it?"

"Peter." Helen smiles. "The guards won't know how they fell asleep. We'll be gone before they wake, and they will be far too afraid of the king to say anything about it. Especially since Berk will still be there. No harm done."

"Why can't we take Berk and find the way out?"

"They won't be asleep that long. And there are still the guards outside. We'd need more drugs."

I want to get Berk out of Athens now. But Helen is right. We have no way to escape. Not yet. Alex is working on something. Something that requires me to be kind to the king and pretend he isn't a horrible tyrant. I do not love the plan, but I cannot think of one that would be any better.

"I don't remember which it is." Helen is looking at a wall. It looks no different than the other walls we passed. She touches a few stones. Nothing happens. She steps on a stone at the edge of the wall. The wall shifts. The air smells musty. I cover my mouth to keep from coughing. If this is the holding chamber, then guards are here. I need to remain silent.

"Who's there?" One of the guards heard the wall opening. Helen pulls out her sleeping drug, presses the top, and rolls it toward the sound of the voices.

"Stay back." Helen pulls me against the wall. "It is powerful."

"But Berk?" I don't want to come all this way to watch him sleeping.

"He is behind a wall just like this," Helen whispers. "The only opening is at the top, and the sleeping drug was made to stay low so those under it will continue to breathe it in for the duration."

I hear the sound of a body drop. A guard calls out to the man, and then another body drops. Three more and Helen pulls me through the opening. "Hold your breath until we're in the chamber."

I do as she says, but my lungs burn as she works the chamber's lock. She rushes to one of the guards, removes a tiny card that slides into the lock, and pushes me through the door. We both take deep breaths.

197

"I'm going back into the hallway to keep watch," Helen says. "You have fifteen minutes."

The door slams shut and my eyes cannot adjust to the darkness. I can't see Berk. I can't see anything. But suddenly I feel him. Arms that can only belong to Berk crush me to his chest.

"I don't care if you're a hallucination," he whispers into my ear. He sways slightly, and I realize he can barely stand.

"What have they done to you?" I pull back and feel Berk's face. Slight stubble covers his cheeks, but I can feel scrapes there as well. It is dark in here, the only light coming through the tiny slits around the door frame. As my eyes adjust, I see Berk has been beaten. One of his eyes is swollen shut; the other is framed in blood.

"It's really you?" Berk blinks his good eye and cups my face with his hands.

"Yes." All thoughts of our fight, my jealousy, are gone. This is Berk—my friend, my playmate and confidant. He is hurt and imprisoned because of me. I want to yell at him and hug him at the same time. "Have you been hallucinating me?"

Berk smiles, but I can see even that is painful. "One time you broke through the wall in one of those cars they pull."

"I broke through the wall?" I laugh at the image. "That wall?"

"Right through." Berk motions with his head toward the stones behind him. "Didn't even get messy."

"Your first clue that it was a hallucination?"

"No. My first clue was that I was floating when you broke through."

I step back. "Now that would have been something to see."

"Why are you here?" Berk's smile fades. "Is this the final visit before they execute me?"

"No. No, of course not!"

"I didn't expect to live through this." Berk takes my hands. "I just wanted to try to save you."

"And I want to save you." I squeeze his hands.

"I'm sorry, Thalli." He lets go of my hands. "I've spent every moment since you left wishing I could take back what I said. If something happened to you—I don't know what I would have done."

"I'm sorry too, Berk."

"John and I spent a lot of time talking while you were gone." Berk steps away and looks at me. "He taught me about the verses he gave you."

"'The Lord is my shepherd'?"

"I have been praying that the Designer would set a table before you in the presence of our enemies."

I glance around. "He has."

Berk leans against the wall. He is weary. "I'm sorry."

"Why are you sorry now?"

"I should have thought through this more." Berk sighs. "But you had been gone so long. I was worried. The ten days were up, and Carey was talking Gerald into two weeks. I couldn't stand it. I was sure you were hurt. I was going to come like you did, as a refugee. But when the guard greeted me outside the gate and told me you were marrying the prince, I couldn't think clearly. I just ran."

"That was quite an entrance you made." I shake my head. "Always trying to rescue me."

"Did he hurt you?" Berk's voice is quiet. "That prince. Did he . . . do anything to you?"

"No. Alex is a good man. He is going to help us. He's part of the plan."

"Are you sure you can trust him?"

"Yes." I hear feet along the hallway outside.

"We have to go," Helen whispers through the door.

"That's his sister."

"His sister?"

"I'll tell you all about it later." I move toward the door. "When I come to save you."

"I guess I *am* the one needing rescuing." Berk laughs. "I'll stay clear of the wall."

I don't want to leave, but I recall what Helen said. If the guards wake and don't know what happened, they won't do anything. But if they wake and see us here . . . I don't even want to think about what could happen.

"I'll be back for you." I walk out the door, past the guards, praying that I can do just that.

CHAPTER THIRTY-EIGHT

I can't open the door to my room.

I tried pushing against it, banging on it. I screamed for Helen, for Alex, for a guard. Nothing. I cannot climb out the window. It is too high. I have pressed every stone on the walls and the floor like I saw Helen do, hoping there is a secret entrance here. Nothing. I am trapped.

Something very bad is happening. I am no longer a guest, but a prisoner. Like Berk. And if I am a prisoner like Berk, I cannot help him.

I fall onto the bed. My throat is raw from screaming. My muscles ache from pushing against the wall and running around the room. I don't understand what is happening, and I hate that more than anything.

I must have fallen asleep again because the next time I open my eyes, the room is brighter. Sunlight filters through the red curtains, making the room appear to be bleeding. I jump up, praying that I was dreaming earlier, that I am not locked in. But it was not a dream. The door is immobile. My hands still hurt from banging on it. I lean my back against the door and slide down.

"Thalli?" I barely hear the whisper.

"Alex?"

"Shh." A sheet of yellowed paper slides under the door, and I open it. "Father knows of your visit last night. The chamber is filled with surveillance equipment. Stay quiet and say nothing else. I will do everything I can to help you and Berk."

I gasp. I want to throw a chair against the door, race down to the prison chamber. I want to rescue Berk just like he dreamed—breaking through a wall, floating out of Athens. But I am powerless. And the king is angry. He knows about our visit. He heard what we said. He knows Helen and Alex are part of our plan to rescue Berk. I have placed so many lives in danger. I want to cry and scream, but I will do what Alex asked: stay quiet.

I sit on the bed and try not to think about what the king will do with this information, of what Alex has to protect me from. Instead I think about Berk trapped below. I think of Helen, caring enough for me to help me see Berk. As we walked back last night, she smiled more than I have ever seen her smile. I wanted to ask her more about Peter and her. I could tell she was thinking about him. I pray there will be a future for Peter and

Helen. I will do everything I can to bring them back together, to give Helen a life full of happiness, of freedom. She does not deserve to be trapped here, mistreated by this king who would kill her mother and plot to kill her.

But I can do nothing while I am trapped in this room, waiting for whatever punishment the king has planned for me. My only hope is that he still wants to put on the show of a wedding, still wants the people to love me so he can kill me and incite the people against New Hope. At least that will give me more time to find a way to help Berk and Helen escape.

A soft knock sounds on the door. Alex has returned. "Thalli."

That is not Alex's voice. I walk to the door. "Yes?"

"It's Carey."

My heart drops. Carey is in Athens too? "Why . . . ?"

"We knew something happened when Berk did not return." Carey is not trying to keep his voice quiet. He didn't sneak in here. Of course not. What price did he pay to enter the city? I cannot even bear to think of it. "Kristie and I are here to try to negotiate for your release."

I close my eyes. "I am sorry."

"Don't apologize. We sent you here knowing the dangers. We allowed Berk to come too. We should have known better."

"What about Gerald?" Suddenly I find myself wanting nothing more than to see the old man leading his army into battle against the king.

"The guard met us outside the city." Carey's voice is low. He is holding something back.

"What happened?"

"The Athenian army made it clear they are more powerful than New Hope's army."

There is so much more I want to ask—were they hurt? killed? captured? But I cannot ask that now. And clearly, Carey does not want to share the details with me. "What can I do?"

"The king has called for a trial. You, Berk, and Helen will be placed on the stand."

"What about Alex?"

"He is testifying against you."

"*What?*" I press my hands against the door. Surely I heard wrong.

"He and his father planned the trial."

"No." I look at the note still in my hand. *I will do everything I can to help you and Berk.* I will not believe Alex turned against me, deceived me. He must be pretending to aid his father in order to help us.

"I have been given permission to represent you. I will meet with you in one hour. The guards will release you from your room and bring you to me. I need to know everything that has happened. Anything that would help me clear your name."

If the king is making us stand trial, he will not allow himself to lose. He is simply bringing us forward so we can condemn ourselves in front of the people. Or worse, he is planning to use us to bring condemnation on New Hope.

"Thalli, did you hear what I said?"

"Yes." If surveillance devices are here, I do not want anything potentially incriminating to come out of my mouth. I will keep these thoughts to myself.

"John sent this for you." Another slip of paper slides under the door. I can barely read the writing. John uses an ancient script and his hands are shaky. It takes me several minutes to decipher it.

"Be strong and of good courage; do not be afraid, nor be dismayed, for the Lord your God is with you wherever you go."

I read the words and calm washes over me. I can trust the Designer in this. John is right. I move away from the door. I step into the bathing chamber and imagine I am rinsing away my fear with the water, putting on courage with my clothes.

By the time the guard comes, I am ready. I do not know what awaits me, what waits for Berk or Helen. I do not know if Alex is working for or against me. But I do know that the Lord my God is with me wherever I go.

CHAPTER THIRTY-NINE

Death is not a sufficient sentence."

The king has been talking for thirty minutes. Thirty minutes without a pause. This is not a trial. It is a demonstration of his power. And it is, as I feared, his plan to incite the people against New Hope. We were dragged out here in front of everyone, our hands restrained behind our backs, guards positioned behind us.

"Thalli deceived us. She claimed to come from the State, when in reality she came from New Hope. She claimed to seek refuge, but she was actually seeking to destroy us. She claimed to care for my son—your prince—but those feelings were as false as her story."

No one speaks. They do not even shout their approval. These people have obviously been conditioned to remain deathly silent when the king is speaking.

"Thalli took advantage of our hospitality . . . she took advantage of our prince." The king gazes at Alex, a blank look on his face, sitting beside him.

Alex has only looked at me once since the trial began. He, who never stopped looking at me whenever we were together, is avoiding my gaze. I am beginning to wonder if he really is on the king's side. I pray that is not true. I thought he cared for me. That he was good. But I cannot forget he is this king's son. This wicked, heartless, murderous king. Maybe Alex is like his father. I recall our time together, his kind words, his care and protection. Is he capable of that kind of deception? And if he is, am I so naive that I fell victim to it?

"She mocks me and you. She mocks Athens. And for what? For whom? For the wicked people of New Hope."

The king is silent. I glance around and the people's eyes are wide with fear. What do they believe about New Hope? I want to jump up, shout to them that everything they are being told is ridiculous. But I bite my lip. Speaking will do no good. So I pray.

"She infiltrates our city, brings in an accomplice." The king motions to Berk who is strapped to a chair on the platform below the king. "And she makes her malicious plans even as we welcome her into our homes, into our families."

Hundreds of gazes lock on me, following the king's lead. They are angry, fearful. They believe everything he says.

"She has even turned my own daughter into a traitor." The king glares at Helen, sitting beside Alex on the platform. She is sitting straight, but fear clouds her eyes. She does not deserve this. I am guilty of deception. The king is right about that. But Helen is guilty of nothing but kindness to a stranger, of believing in love.

"If we simply execute these lawbreakers, the people of New Hope will send others. They will not rest until they accomplish their goal."

The people nod. I look closer at the crowd, and I see guards walking among them, with small contraptions in their hands. They are always moving, one hand on the tops of the contraptions. It is a drug. This is how they are controlling the people, keeping them quiet.

I gaze at Berk, my eyes wide. But he is affected as well. He looks through me, not at me, and his stare, like Alex's, is blank. I want to rip my hands out of these restraints, shove the guards aside, and grab Berk away, shake Alex out of this mindlessness. But even my slight movement forward on the chair causes one of the guards to advance.

Carey, Kristie, and I are on a platform several feet above the crowd, across from the king's platform. I glance behind me. Our guards have no contraptions. I wonder why.

"We will give these lawbreakers an opportunity to defend themselves." The king points to us. "Then we will determine their fate."

Carey stands. The muscle in his jaw is tense. "People of Athens, what your king says is untrue. We mean you no harm. We want to live peaceably with you—"

"Then why send a spy here? Why trick my son into an engagement and sneak another man here to stop the wedding?"

I jump up from my seat. "You announced my engagement without even consulting me!"

"You dare to contradict me?" the king bellows, and the people begin to get agitated.

Carey places a hand on my arm. "You have allowed us to speak in Thalli and Berk's defense. May we continue?"

"You may speak in their defense." The king leans forward. "But you may not speak lies to my people. They will not tolerate that."

The people nod furiously. Their gazes dart from the king's platform to ours. The guards continue to move among them.

"Then you should follow your own decrees." Carey is yelling now, his hands punctuating every word. "Speak truth to these people. Tell them how you have been seeking to destroy New Hope for years. How you hurt innocent people, steal from us, how you refused to negotiate when we attempted a peaceful solution to the problems *you* began!"

"Silence! You see why we must take seriously this threat against us? They wish to destroy us and our way of life. Even when faced with execution, they defend their lies. This must not be allowed to continue."

The people nod at the king. They move closer to him. This is exactly what he wanted. This is why they were drugged and we were not. He wanted us to get angry. He wanted the people to see it and manipulate our anger to his advantage.

I turn and see one of the guards standing close behind me. Too close. I hold my breath. I will not be drugged. I will fight him before I take in one more lungful of Athens' pharmaceuticals. But he does not carry a drugging contraption with him. He carries a weapon. He steps behind Kristie and points the weapon at her head.

I feel like the world suddenly stops moving. He is going to

kill Kristie right here on this platform. I stand but I lose my balance because my arms are pinned behind my back. I cannot do anything. The guard looks at me and reaches for a button on the side of his weapon.

"No!" I shove my body into his. A deafening sound causes me to freeze.

I am too late.

CHAPTER FORTY

My daughter." The king's voice is still magnified, but he is no longer yelling.

Kristie is not injured. The guard has rushed down from the platform. The weapon is beside Kristie.

"She killed my daughter." The king begins to wail—an unnatural sound. It takes me a few moments before what he says registers. I look at the platform where Helen was sitting. She is no longer in her chair. The king is standing over her body. Bright red blood flows from a wound in her chest.

Helen is dead.

I stare at Kristie and Carey. Their eyes are wide.

The people follow the king's example. They begin wailing, screaming. They raise their fists at me, rush toward me.

"Stop." The king addresses the people. They are all silent. "We will not give these murderers the satisfaction of a quick death. They will not be excused so easily."

The king wipes tears from his eyes, and the people do the same. "Please give my son and me time to say good-bye to my daughter. Return to your homes and wait for further instructions. Guards, confine these prisoners to the lowest level of our prison chamber. Protect yourselves against them. Protect us from them. We cannot allow them to do any more harm to the good people of Athens."

I feel my elbows pressed together behind me. I cry out as a new set of restraints is fastened so tightly to my wrists it tears the skin.

"This is nothing compared to what will happen to you," the guard holding on to me growls into my ear, his breath rancid.

"Thalli—" Kristie tries to turn toward me, but another guard places a knee in her back and she crumples to the ground.

Carey tries to reach for his wife, but he is also subdued. The three of us are dragged back into the palace through a side door that leads to a small transport that takes us below the main floor. Far below it. When the doors of the transport open, we are in a dark, narrow hallway. The walls are made from a different material than the rest of the palace. They are chalky and dusty. Cobwebs block our way and the guards push us through them. The sticky webs cover my eyelashes and my nose. I cannot move my hands, so I have to leave them there.

I try to rub my face against my shoulder, but the guard behind me shoves me down. I fall into Carey's back and we both tumble to the hard floor. I land on Carey. Without the use of his hands to stop his fall, his head bangs hard against the floor. He doesn't move.

"Carey." I try to roll off him, to nudge him with my elbow, but a guard pulls me into a standing position by my restraints and walks right on top of Carey.

"No." Kristie is behind us. She can barely speak, barely walk. She is too old to be treated like this. Carey is too. They won't survive this treatment.

"Take the girl," a guard shouts. "I'll peel this one off the floor and put him and the old lady in together."

"Shouldn't we separate them?" the guard by me asks, his voice echoing off the narrow walls.

"The old guy might be dead already." The guard laughs. It is a horrible sound. "If he's not, it won't be long. Having him in with her will be a good reminder for the lady to do what we say."

The guard shoves me against the wall. Dirt is ground into my pores. I didn't shut my mouth in time, and a gritty substance on the wall falls into my throat. I cough, and the guard only pushes me harder.

"Quit it, or you'll end up just like your friend there." His breath makes my eyes water. "If I didn't believe the king wanted you alive, I'd kill you myself."

I am thrown into a cell, right into a sleeping platform. It hits me below my knees, and I turn myself so I land on my back and not my face. My head still slams into the hard platform, and I am momentarily stunned.

The door closes and I am in complete darkness. Complete silence. It is then that the image of Helen lying bleeding on the platform sinks into my consciousness.

Helen is dead. She wanted only to escape. To be reunited with Peter. To be loved. She helped me, risked her life for me. And her life was taken from her.

The sickening reality of the farce of a trial rushes in vivid color to my mind: The king planned everything. The drugs, our response. He even orchestrated his own daughter's death. Not only our deaths, but also the deaths of all the people of New Hope. Did he know I would try to see Berk? That Helen would help? Did he instruct the guards to let us walk down that hallway? Was he watching all of it, a sadistic grin plastered on his face as all his plans were coming together?

Tears slip from my eyes, past the cobwebs that surround them. I cannot stop them. What will the king convince the people to do next? What can I do?

"Thalli." Kristie's voice sounds like it is coming from a hundred miles away.

"Are you okay?" I shout into the darkness. "Is Carey all right?"

"Carey is unconscious, but he is alive."

"I'm sorry." I rub my face with my shoulder, but the tears refuse to stop.

"There is nothing you could have done. We were all set up. I should have known."

"Where is Berk?" He was not taken away with us. He was next to Helen. Drugged. I tried to see him in the moments after the weapon discharged, but the crowd was too thick. I recall seeing the king, but I do not recall seeing Berk. Where was he?

"I don't know."

"What do we do?"

"Wait," Kristie says, her voice a whisper in the darkness. "We just wait."

CHAPTER FORTY-ONE

feel like I have been in this cell for weeks. In reality, I suppose it has only been a day or two. But there is no light, and we have been given no food. The air is stale, fetid with the stench of my inability to control my own bodily functions. My lips are so dry, they are bleeding. I cannot speak anymore. Kristie has not spoken for far too long. I have yelled for her, cried out for her. Nothing. I pray she has been taken away, that she is not lying in there with Carey, their cell a death chamber.

I recall the last time I was plunged into darkness. I was undergoing cerebral testing back in the State. Something went wrong, and I lost my eyesight. I was terrified. But Berk was there, letting me know with a touch that he was with me.

Sometimes I'm sure that is where I am again. That all this has been part of the testing. That Dr. Loudin is watching from his laboratory. And sometimes, I hope that is true. I would prefer life in the State to this. I would allow Dr. Loudin to do any kind of testing on me he wishes. I would prefer the annihilation chamber, with its kind gas lulling me to sleep as I watch the image of a garden and feel its breeze on my face.

Sometimes I am sure I hear Berk talking to me. He is beside me, but I cannot touch him. He tells me he will come for me. He will break through the wall and we will escape and everything will be fine.

I don't know if those are dreams or hallucinations. But they are not reality. The reality is I am living in a dark cell with little oxygen and no help. My rescuers are dead or dying. Helen is dead. Alex . . . I have had dreams about Alex too. Sometimes he is coming to rescue me. Other times he is with his father, part of the grand plan to destroy New Hope, thanking me for making that plan a reality.

I try to recall the words John taught me, the words he sent about being strong and courageous. But I cannot be strong and courageous. I am so very afraid. And so alone.

"Get up, girl." The door opens and the light from a torch the guard carries makes my eyes burn. It is so bright. "Get up."

I roll to my side, try to use my elbows to lift myself into a sitting position. But I cannot. I have no strength. What little I might have had was extinguished by the blinding light.

I feel a strong hand at my shoulder, propelling me up. I cry out from the pain of his grip, but he does not release me until I am on my feet. I fall forward and the guard catches me. My eyes are closed, but I can see the glow from the torch in front of my eyelids.

"You stink." His breath is hot on my face. If I had energy, I would tell him that at least I have an excuse for my odor. But I do not have energy. And I am hurting all over. I cannot risk being hurt more.

"She needs to bathe." The guard pushes me so far that I am forced to open my eyes so I can see where I am going. But the light is too bright. All I see is red. And then I land on a hard surface. One that smells terrible. Another guard. He pushes me away from him.

"I'll take her to Melitta." The guard keeps his palms against my back, pushing me ahead of him.

We walk through the hallway. I open my eyes a millimeter at a time until I can open them all the way without them burning and watering. I am filthy. The chamber I was in must have been covered in black dirt, because that is all over my arms and my clothes. There are holes in my pants from where I hit the sleeping platform, and there is a rip down the side from where I rubbed against the wall, trying to hear from Kristie.

I want to ask for water, but I am too frightened to speak. And I am sure that even if I tried, nothing would come out. I don't even know how I am able to keep one foot moving in front of the other.

"Take her." We have reached a room carved out of the chalky walls. It is moist and smells of soap.

"I clean laundry, not prisoners." The woman at the far end of the room is middle aged, with wiry black hair sprinkled with white strands. Her face is prematurely wrinkled, and she is missing most of her teeth.

"You do what you're told or you'll end up a prisoner yourself." The woman dumps a silver tub filled with water into a receptacle in the wall and places it under a faucet. Clear water runs out and fills up the tub. The guard leaves.

"Get undressed."

"I cannot." I glance behind me. The restraints keep my arms pinned behind me.

The woman rolls her eyes. "You think I am so stupid that I would remove those for you? So you could kill me like you killed the princess?"

I want to defend myself, but each word is painful, and this woman wouldn't believe me anyway.

"Be still." The woman has a large pair of scissors in her hand. She places them at my neck and cuts my clothing off me. She digs the sharp ends of the scissors into my skin every time she opens them, but I am too exhausted to cry out. I watch the water flowing into the tub and imagine myself drinking from it.

Soon I am in the tub. The water is cold, but I don't care. The water turns dark brown as the dirt slides off my skin. I get a mouthful of the running water before the woman turns the faucet off. I swallow it slowly, allowing the cool liquid to soothe my raging throat. I want to scrub every inch of my body with the thickest cloth I can find. But I don't have use of my arms, so all I can do is rub my legs together and wipe my face against my shoulder.

"All I have is laundry soap." The woman drops a huge block of soap into the water.

"Can you help me?" I cannot even see the soap in the filthy water.

The woman sighs. "Fine." She grabs a coarse cloth and scrubs my hair with so much force, I am sure every strand will come out in her hands. She then shoves my head underwater. I am unprepared, and water goes burning into my nose. I come up and cough, and she shoves me down again.

"Enough." The woman holds up a drying cloth that looks as rough as the walls. I lean forward, positioning myself on my knees and dragging myself up to my feet. She throws the cloth around my shoulders and I step out of the tub, freezing and humiliated.

The guard pokes his head into the room. "You done yet?"

"Almost." The woman pulls a brown shirt and pants from a pile of clothing on a counter. "How am I supposed to dress her with her arms tied behind her back?"

"Throw the shirt over her." The guard's voice sounds like a trombone with a battered horn. "She won't be needing her arms."

The woman complies. She is rough, the material is rough, but it's clean and it smells of soap. So I choose to give thanks for these small mercies. Once I am dressed, the guard grabs my shoulder and once again propels me forward.

"Where . . . ?" I clear my throat and try to bring the words out. "Where are you taking me?"

"To the king. He's been preparing something special for you." The guard says these words with a horrible laugh, and my blood freezes.

Death, I can handle. I was prepared before, thanks to John. Death does not frighten me.

Dying, however, is terrifying.

CHAPTER FORTY-TWO

smell what I am sure is burning flesh. It is a horrible smell. If anything was in my stomach, I am sure I would lose it all. But there is nothing, so I gag and retch, my throat screaming in pain. But I cannot help it.

I close my eyes as we walk into the open. I do not want to see who is burning. It will be one of my friends. Carey, Kristie . . . Berk. I am not courageous enough to watch any of them burn. I do not even have any tears left to spend on them, but my heart breaks with every step.

There are punishments worse than death. The king knows this. He will force me to watch each of my friends die before he kills me. I am sure of this.

I expect to hear the sound of people cheering as I enter—the cheers of those happy to see a condemned person facing her fate. But instead I hear wailing, sobbing, sounds of grief. The heat of a fire warms my face, and I dare to open my eyes. I was right. It is one of my friends being burned. But not the one I expected.

Helen.

This must be their funeral rite. I recall reading about those in history lessons. The ancients had a variety of ways to dispose of the dead. Burning, in the opinion of the State, was the most effective. This was not an incinerator, though. This was a tall pile of wood, with jewels and gold mixed in. Helen lay on top surrounded by flames, dressed like royalty.

I do not want to watch, but I cannot turn away. This is my fault. I did not discharge the weapon, but I am the cause of its discharge. The king wanted to start a war, and he used Helen to do it. Knowing he planned this before I came along does not ease the guilt I feel. What if we had run away earlier? Taken Berk when we infiltrated his cell and just ran? Would she have survived? What if the guard had missed? What if I grabbed him before he could take aim?

None of this seems fair. Helen deserved to live. She deserved to be with Peter and have a life of love and peace.

I cannot breathe, my throat is so tight. It feels like someone has stuffed a stone deep inside it. Stones line my throat, go down into my heart. I know loss. I have experienced it before. But this is so much more. So much worse.

I am falling, black spots dancing in front of my eyes. I feel the guard grab my shoulder, but he cannot catch me. I do not hit the ground. Instead I float up, up. I see Helen from above the flames. So far above, I don't even feel the heat. She is crying, burning, begging me to save her. But I cannot reach her. I am caught above just like I was caught below.

"Please, Thalli." Flames hide her face. She is in torment. "Help me. Help me."

I cannot move. My arms are pinned behind me. My feet are frozen.

Then I am drowning. Water fills my mouth, my nose, my eyes. I want the water to fall onto Helen. I do not need it. She needs it. I try to tell whoever is submerging me to help Helen. But I cannot speak.

"You will wake up."

I open my eyes to see the face of a guard looming over me, his breath hot and foul in my face.

I passed out. The guard threw water on me to wake me. He pulls me back onto my feet, but I sway, my ears ringing. I cannot stand. My legs will not hold me.

"Leave her on the ground," another voice shouts. "Do not let her behavior direct attention away from the princess."

"Of course." The guard looks above at the fire, leaving me half sitting, half lying on the ground.

I breathe in and out slowly, carefully, trying to bring enough oxygen into my lungs to prevent myself from fainting again. As terrible as this reality is, my dreams while unconscious were even worse.

I look beyond Helen, to the platform where she was killed, and I see the king and Alex. The king is expressionless. Alex is not. His face shows a mixture of grief and anger. His stare is locked on Helen's burning form. I cannot imagine what he is thinking. He lost his mother, now his sister. His only remaining family is the king, who ordered the murders of those who died.

His gaze finds mine. I want to communicate concern to him, but when he looks at me, I see hatred. Pure, burning hatred, directed right at me. He speaks to his father, points to me. The king nods and whispers something to a guard standing beside him. That guard walks toward us.

I try to catch Alex's gaze again. Surely he does not believe I killed Helen. Surely he realizes this was the king's actions, his plan. But as I continue to watch him, I see that his eyes are clouded, blank. His is the look of one who has been drugged.

"The king has ordered that the prisoner be removed," the king's guard says.

"Very well." My guard glances toward the king. "Do I return her to the chamber?"

"No." The guard glares at me, hatred blazing in his eyes as well. "The trial begins when the funeral ends. Go put her with the others."

The guard pushes me forward, away from the fire and the platform. We walk toward a rectangular tower that stands out from the main palace. The door opens and my guard stops. "The orders are for her to stay here until the trial."

"Fine." A guard inside speaks, but I cannot see him. No lights illuminate this place. My eyes cannot adjust quickly to the changes.

I feel a hand on my shoulder, and I am pushed into a room that smells like the laundry room. But there is no moisture here. High up, a window allows just a tiny slice of sunlight in. I see shadows at first. Then I hear a door slam.

"Thalli?" Berk. I know his voice, but I still see only shadows. "You're alive."

I feel Berk near me. His arms are bound also, but we lean

223

against each other. He has been cleaned, like me. I smell the laundry soap on his coarse clothes. I want to wrap my arms around him, to touch his face. But I am content to hear his heartbeat. To know he is alive.

"What did they do to you?" Fear invades Berk's voice.

"I am all right." I step back, look at Berk until his features become clear. His face isn't as bruised as the last time I saw him. His scratches are healing. The stubble on his cheeks has grown into the beginnings of a beard. "They left me alone."

Berk sighs. "Good."

"Carey and Kristie?" I look around. "Are they—?"

"They were allowed to leave."

"What?"

"The king released them. He even gave them transport back to New Hope."

My mind races. Why would he do that? They were next to me. I heard Kristie shouting. I did not hear guards take them away. Perhaps I was sleeping when it happened. "Are you sure?"

"I saw them go. I was held in a room above this one. I watched out the window as they left."

"They will tell the people what happened," I say, the pieces coming together. "They will bring others."

"I know." Berk closes his eyes. "I tried to call out to them as they left. I wanted to warn them. But they didn't hear me."

"They are wise." I swallow hard. "They know the king. They saw the lengths he will go to, to deceive his people. They will not walk into a trap."

"I would." Berk sighs again.

"What?"

"If I knew you were in danger, I would come." Berk gazes at

me, his green eyes full of emotion. "Even knowing I'd be walking to my death."

And I realize that is exactly what he did. "Let us hope Carey and Kristie aren't as emotional as we are."

CHAPTER FORTY-THREE

How dare you allow them to be together!" Alex's voice pierces the room. I hear a guard being slammed to the ground. "They conspired to murder the princess. Who knows what other atrocities they have planned. They get no mercy. Nothing. Do you understand?"

The guard grunts. "Sorry, Your Majesty. I was not aware."

"You are fortunate I came," Alex says. "They would likely have killed you and escaped."

"Yes, sir." Fear fills the guard's voice. "Thank you, sir."

Alex's frame fills the doorway. I never noticed how tall he is, how muscular. How frightening.

"Alex." I want to break through the drugs he is under. I want to find the Alex I know. "Please listen."

"I have listened enough." Alex looks at me, his eyes a dark blue, darker than I have ever seen them, the whites of his eyes tinged with red—from tears? From the fire? From the drugs? "I befriended you. I believed you. I cared for you. And you used me."

"No, Alex." I take a step toward him. He holds his arm out, palm up.

"No more." Alex lowers his arm, but the message is clear: Stay back. Keep quiet. "Father is right. About everything. My weakness cost Helen her life. I will not be weak again."

Berk looks at me. He closes his eyes, lifts his chin. *Pray.* We cannot save ourselves. We cannot convince Alex of our innocence. We can do nothing. But we are not without hope.

I am reminded of a story John told me once, about three men who were thrown into a fire by a wicked king. These men were righteous, and they were sentenced to death because of that. But the Designer saved them. They did not burn. In fact, when the king looked into the fire, he saw not three men, but four. The Designer was with them.

Thank you. Peace and calm fill me. The Designer has helped people in this position before. He will help us.

Alex leaves and the guard takes Berk, moves him to the room above. I am alone again. But I am not alone. I feel the presence of the Designer. I think of him when the guard comes in with bread and milk. He feeds me, stuffing the food into my mouth, pouring the liquid into my throat. But it is a table prepared for me in the presence of my enemy. I will not fear.

The guard leaves and I lie down. The food—the first I've

had in so long—makes me tired. I rest, dreaming now. Not of
Helen burning and Berk rescuing, but of green pastures and
still waters.

"The king is ready for you." The guard is once again above
me. "Come."

The light is bright and the crowd is angry, but I refuse to
allow fear to win. I will walk through the valley of the shadow
of death and fear no evil.

:: :: ::

I am on the platform. Berk is here too, but we are not allowed
to see each other. Two guards stand between us. The king and
Alex are in front of us, looking out over the crowd. The remains
of the fire that consumed Helen's body are beside us. The acrid
smell of burnt flesh and the sweet smell of smoldering wood
fill the air.

Hundreds of people look up at the king. No drugs are necessary to keep them quiet, to keep them subdued. The death of
the princess has done that. They do not know—nor will they
believe—that the princess was not the king's daughter, that
the king had his own wife murdered, Helen's father murdered,
and Helen herself murdered. If we even attempted to say those
truths, the people would surely come up and kill us with their
own hands. They blindly follow this king, despite his ruthless-
ness, his lies. He rules through a lethal combination of fear
and pharmaceuticals. Like the Scientists in the State, he seeks
to control his people by whatever means are at his disposal.
And he justifies it with the belief that given true freedom, the
people would destroy themselves.

What kind of world would I like, were I given the choice? How much power would I give people? How much power would I give the rulers? I think of the Designer and I know that no matter what, if his ways are not considered, no State or city or government will be truly successful. Even New Hope struggles to make right decisions, fights against prejudices and fear. Is perfection even possible?

I look up and see three guards standing on the city walls. They are directly above the gate. The guard in the center holds a white flag above his head. What does that mean? I look at the king and see he is watching those guards as well. He stares at the white flag for a long moment. To the people, he likely appears to be deep in thought, gazing out at the horizon, remembering his daughter.

"People of Athens." The king breaks the silence, his voice quieter than normal. "It is not customary to hold a trial so soon after a royal funeral. But there is nothing customary in any of the events of the last few days."

The people nod, and some wipe tears from their eyes. Many glance at where Helen had lain, compassion etched on their faces.

"This crime, however, is so heinous, these criminals so dangerous, that I felt we had no choice but to hold this trial now. With you all here, as both jury and eyewitnesses."

The people clap, a slow, somber clap. The king accepts it, arms stretched out toward the people, a sad smile on his face.

"Today we mourn together the loss of our princess." The king wipes a tear that does not exist from his face. The citizens see what they want in that gesture—real tears, real compassion. "And we seek to bring justice to those who killed her."

The clapping is louder this time. The king allows it to continue for a full minute before raising his hands to stop it.

"I have stood here too often lately." The king shakes his head. "Introducing you to the woman we believed would marry our prince. Bringing that same woman before you as a traitor and spy. Now I stand, a grieving father, once again bringing this woman, Thalli, before you as a murderer."

The crowd utters a collective hiss, every eye on me, condemning me.

"Because of the heinousness of her crime, we will not allow Thalli to speak in her defense, nor will we allow her accomplice, Berk, to do so. We have seen they speak only lies. We have also seen that as long as they live, our lives are in danger."

The people nod. The king once again looks out to where the white flag waves in the wind.

"I dictate death by fire." The king motions toward the edge of the city. "Not here, where our princess was mourned, but on the outskirts. I recommend Berk burn first while Thalli watches."

Even though I suspected this, the reality of it hits me with a force that weakens my legs. To watch Berk die—burn to death—is worse than facing my own execution.

I look up and see the white flag replaced with a black one. The king smiles so slightly, I am sure I'm the only one who notices.

"And I recommend we go immediately." The king's voice grows in strength. "Any objections?"

The crowd is silent.

Our deaths have been decreed.

CHAPTER FORTY-FOUR

One would think that after several near-death experiences, I would no longer be moved by them.

One would be wrong.

I am walking behind the king, with a guard on each side of me, like I am a dangerous criminal who, even as she walks to her execution, is capable of one more murder. Of course, that is exactly what the king wants the crowd to think.

The reality is, I am so weak I can barely walk, much less think. I am using every ounce of energy in my body to keep going. But I will keep going. I will not die as a weakling. I will walk to my death. I will not be carried or helped in any way. The king may accuse me of the worst, but I know the truth, the

Designer knows the truth, and John has told me the truth sets me free. So I will go to my death free.

There is a commotion behind us. A guard rides up on a horse through the crowd, right up to the king. The entire procession pauses as the guard speaks in low tones and the king's eyes lower as he hears the news. With a nod to the king, the guard returns to his horse, reverses the large animal, and rides back out the way he came. The king says nothing, but with a wave of his hand, commands the crowd to continue the march to the outskirts of town.

I do not know what was said, but it appears the king was expecting it. He did not react with anger, frustration, or impatience.

I wish I could walk with Berk, be near him. But we are separated by a dozen guards. I wonder what he is thinking. Is he wishing we had stayed in the State? Is he wondering if saving me from the annihilation chamber was worth it?

But John and Rhen are in New Hope, safe for now. They will live on, thrive, help that community. It was worth escape for that. For the extra time we had together, for the knowledge that the State was not the lone survivor of the War. There are other cities, here and in other parts of the earth, where people survived. I am glad I know that, saw that.

I feel more prepared to meet the Designer than I did in the annihilation chamber. I know him better. I have seen him more. I was ready then, but I am even more ready, even more confident in him now. He could choose to save me, like he did before. But even if he doesn't, I believe heaven awaits. And John says there is no pain in heaven, no sadness. No separation. I want to go there.

Even the sky seems dark—unusually dark for this time of day. Like it is mourning with us. The breeze carries moisture on it. I close my eyes and allow its coolness to refresh me.

The guards around me stop. I cannot see past them. They are a wall in front of me, all much taller than I, standing shoulder to shoulder. Guards are posted behind me and beside me as well.

"Bring the prisoners to me," the king says.

A guard beside me takes my elbow and presses me forward. The guards in front of us part, giving me a clear view of the king. And Alex. They both stand on a platform that appears newly constructed. It is made from a synthetic wood and stands only six feet off the ground. Beside that, a huge post rises from the ground. It is made of metal and real wood surrounds it. My arms burn with the thought of it. The metal pole will melt our skin long before the fire from the wood kills us. It will be an excruciating death.

And I have to watch Berk endure it before me.

Please, Father. I pray harder than I have ever prayed before. *Do not make us suffer this. Please.*

I am standing in front of the king. He looks at me. I return his stare. He knows the truth, even if the others refuse to listen or cannot believe it. He knows exactly what he has done. And I know it too. He may kill me, but he will kill me knowing I am aware of just how evil he is.

The king looks away first. His gaze sweeps the people. "Arrogant, even in the face of death. Further confirmation that execution is necessary."

The crowd whispers their approval.

"And where did she get these ideas?" The king's voice rises

and falls like the waves in the ocean simulation I saw back in the State. "She got them from our enemies: the citizens of New Hope. There she and others devised how best to trick us, manipulate us, use us in an attempt to gain power over us. There she plotted our deaths. Had she been allowed to continue her plan, Alex would have been killed next. On their honeymoon, no less. And she would have returned and killed me. And then? They would make Athenians the slaves of New Hope. They would use our technology for themselves, however they saw fit. They would destroy us and our way of life. I am thankful they were caught before that happened. But I am heartbroken that my dear Helen was lost before these facts came to light."

My heart is hammering in my chest. If the people would just think, they would see how ridiculous this is. If we planned to take over Athens, why would I have killed Helen so openly? Surely Alex sees through this. But when I look at him, I see he does not. He is blinded, either by the drugs or by love for his father or grief over his sister. Or a combination of all three.

"We see now the lengths to which these barbarians from New Hope will go to achieve their desires." The king scans the crowd. "We see now the need to defend ourselves against them."

Several people shout and echoes follow. The king remains silent and allows the crowd to encourage one another in their hatred for their "enemies."

"We must stand together, then." The king looks out at the crowd. "We must oppose them with all our might. We must protect ourselves against those who would seek our destruction."

The crowd is no longer still. They are agitated, rocking back and forth, shaking their fists. The king accomplished his goal.

I pray for my friends in New Hope. I pray that Kristie and

Carey warned them, perhaps took them from the village to another location. Rhen can help them find another settlement. They are far away, but we traveled hundreds of miles. They can too. I know they can. I pray they escape before the king's army comes after them.

"Tie Berk to the stake." The king doesn't finish the order before the crowd erupts in cheers and applause. They are desperate to see this execution. They are delighted in it. It is sickening.

Berk allows himself to be led to the metal pole. He remains still when his hands are released from the restraints and then placed around the stake. He faces the metal. The guards bind his waist and his legs to the pole so every part of him is touching it. They are maximizing the pain that will be inflicted on him.

Berk looks at me, and we say everything we can in one look. But it is short lived because the guards turn Berk's head away from me. They will give him no solace, no comfort, no mercy in this. They force him to look at the crowd. Those people throw whatever they find at their feet toward Berk—stones, pieces of wood, clumps of dirt. Berk cannot defend himself, and he is hit in his face, his legs, everywhere.

"For the crime of murder," the king shouts and the crowd stills. "You are sentenced to death."

Four guards walk forward, each with a blazing torch in his hands. At the king's command, they lower their torches to the wood. The fire catches immediately, wrapping around Berk's feet, climbing up the pole. Berk's body tenses. I want to close my eyes, but I cannot. I want to save him, but I cannot.

I can do nothing but watch Berk die.

CHAPTER FORTY-FIVE

An explosion rips through the darkening sky. It is so loud, my ears ring.

People from New Hope have come? Remnants from Gerald's army? I am afraid and relieved at the same time. Berk is burning. Dying. I must not be rescued alone.

Another explosion and then . . . water? It feels like tubs full of water are pouring from the sky. So much water that I can barely see in front of me. People are peering around, from the king to Berk to the guards, unsure of what to do.

I think of the three men in the furnace. The Designer walked with them and saved them. He did the same for Berk.

He sent the rain to stop the fire. I gulp in a lungful of air and breathe out my gratitude.

The rain does not last long. But when it subsides, everything and everyone is soaked. The pole where Berk is tied is slick. The wood is covered in a stream of rainwater. Even the king appears less powerful, less intimidating with his tunic stuck to him, revealing a more corpulent figure than is obvious from the layers of clothing he wears. A round belly protrudes and his hair lays in strings along the sides of his head.

But he does not appear defeated. He does not see this as an intervention from the Designer, like the king in John's story did. He does not repent. He looks beyond the crowd toward the city with expectation.

"Your Majesty," a guard shouts from behind us. "An audience has been requested."

"Who would request an audience with the king on this day?" The king's outrage was poorly performed, from my perspective. But the people do not see his hypocrisy. They agree with his words. They are outraged.

"Representatives from New Hope, sir."

I turn and see Kristie, Carey, Rhen, John, and half a dozen other villagers.

"You dare come in *today* and demand an audience?" The king shouts loud enough for even those at the far edges of the crowd to hear. "Today, when my daughter is being laid to rest and her killers are being punished?"

"Her killers are *not* being punished," Carey shouts, and the king has to bang his scepter on the platform to silence the crowd's response.

"Are those two the prisoners I allowed to go free?" The king asks this of the guard beside him, but he does not lower his voice.

"They are, sir." The guard responds with equal volume.

"I show you kindness." The king's face is red as he glares at the older couple. "I allow you to go free because I pity you, because I want you to live out the short time you have left with your people, and this is your repayment?"

"We desire peace," Kristie says. "We do not wish to fight."

"You sent in these spies to murder us!" the king roars. "We will not believe anything you say. You do not want peace."

"These young people were used as pawns by your king," Carey yells. "They no more killed Helen than I did."

The people begin to shout, scream, demand retribution, death to these villagers. The king is triumphant. His eyes glow; his head is high.

"I warned you of these people." He looks at the crowd. "They will stop at nothing to achieve their goals."

The people raise their fists in agreement.

"Therefore, they must be stopped," the king shouts above the crowd. "They must *all* be stopped."

CHAPTER FORTY-SIX

We have been allowed to return to New Hope.

Our restraints have been undone. Guards have walked away from us. The king told the crowd he will not "reward" us with a public death, but he will send us off with the others from New Hope, "to perish corporately." Our crime, he argues, is a result of the planning of the entire village. As such, the whole village must be punished.

We do not speak as we leave. What is there to say? I have seen the arsenal in Athens. Their technology far exceeds that of New Hope. We can try to escape. But the nearest village is so far away. We would need more transports, more food, more time. We lack all of that.

I want to try to speak with Alex, to pull him away from his father's influence, make him understand the truth, to defend us. Alex is good. I have seen it. Berk believes Alex deceived me, that he was part of his father's plan all along. But I refuse to believe that. Berk does not know Alex the way I do. He protected me from his father's wrath. He cares for me. I am sure of it.

"We need Alex." I break the silence, and the entire group looks at me as if I spoke in another language. "The king will not attack us if we have his heir. And once he is no longer under the influence of the Athenian drugs, I know Alex will help us. That was his plan before. We were going to escape to New Hope and help the village protect itself against Athenian attack."

"Thalli." Berk's voice has an edge to it I have never heard before. "You are so sure that Alex was drugged. But isn't it just as likely that you were, and that all the good you think about Alex is a result of that influence?"

I think back on my time in Athens, to my time with Alex. He was kind. I believe that was real. "I heard him defending me to the king, and he did not realize I was listening. He was telling his father *not* to drug me."

Berk steps closer to me. "What happened between you and Alex?"

I stand straight. I do not like his tone, his possessiveness. "I spent time with him—just like you spent time with Rhen."

"That is not the same." Berk's jaw twitches.

"I trust Alex." I look away from Berk but see distrust in Carey's and Kristie's eyes too. "He tried to protect me from his father's plans. He stood up for me against him."

"You don't think they had surveillance on you?" Berk says.

"My guess is they saw you coming to listen at that door and planned the conversation accordingly."

"King Jason is ruthless." Carey shakes his head. "He released Kristie and me, knowing we would return for you. He wanted us to come so he could incite the people against us. I have to agree with Berk. Neither he nor his family is to be trusted."

"What about Helen?" I ask. "She did nothing wrong. She loved Peter—truly loved him—and she helped me. And was killed for the king's purposes."

The events of the last few days have been so draining, I have not truly had time to acknowledge that Helen is dead. My chest feels heavy with the weight of that knowledge. I think of beautiful Helen, hurt by her father, grieving for so much, wanting nothing more than to be free and to love a man of her own choosing. She would want her brother to know the freedom she will never have. She would want me to defend him.

"I know this has been difficult for you." Berk's voice softens. "You should never have gone."

"I had to go." I stop walking, forcing the others to do the same. "And I did it to help New Hope. You needed to know more about Athens and who they are so our village could be better prepared to defend ourselves against them. I did that. I know more about this city than any of you. And our best chance of protecting New Hope is by bringing Alex there."

Kristie and Carey look at each other, then at me. The others in the group glance back at the walls that surround Athens.

"There is a risk in taking him, I realize." I gaze at each person as I speak, willing them to consider what I am saying. "But no greater risk than returning to wait for the Athenian army to attack us."

"No greater risk?" Carey says. "Have you forgotten the prison? Helen? There is huge risk in returning to Athens. You can be sure they are watching us now, making sure we return. I wouldn't be surprised if they aren't tracking our movements. We have no idea all they are capable of."

I consider this. Of course they are watching. Carey is right. But there must be something we can do.

I recall the conversation I had with Helen. "The secret exit. Helen's mother said there is a secret exit at one of the walls."

"Then why didn't she use it?" Berk asks.

"She wasn't sure where it was. And she knew guards were everywhere."

"So the queen and the princess were afraid to use it?"

I do not like the way Berk is speaking to me, as if he thinks I am ignorant. "They had an unhealthy fear of the king."

"Unhealthy?" Berk is yelling now. "Thalli, the man is a murderer. *Their* murderer. Theirs was not an unhealthy fear. It was very healthy."

I will not argue with Berk. He is convinced that he is right. They all are. But I know I need to find that exit. I know I need to get Alex. But I will never be able to convince them.

I walk along in silence. I will go back to New Hope with them. Then while they sleep, I will return to Athens.

CHAPTER FORTY-SEVEN

did not escape. I returned and was surrounded by the people of New Hope. They wanted to know everything. They wanted to debate how to plan for an attack. Somewhere in the middle of the debate, I fell asleep. I did not mean to, but I was more tired than I realized.

I woke up to feel Berk's arms underneath me, carrying me to my quarters. I recalled that I was angry with him, but I was too exhausted to pull myself away. I dreamed I returned to Athens, that I had found the entrance in the wall, that no guards were there. I woke before I found Alex.

John told me the Designer sometimes speaks to his people

through dreams. Was this dream from him? I recall exactly where this spot was. I know just how to get there. I even know how to get in. But it could be just a dream. I could escape only to find myself trapped outside the walls for days. Or worse—I could be caught outside the walls and killed.

I sit up, my head swimming. I ate last night, but I am still so hungry.

"Thalli?" A knock sounds on the door. It is John.

"Come in." I rub my eyes and smooth down my hair.

"I am glad to have you back." John smiles. Despite all the turmoil of the past few weeks, he looks so peaceful. So happy. "You were strong and courageous."

"The Lord prepared a table for me in the presence of my enemies."

John lets out a loud exhale. "Praise be to the Designer."

"Were you here last night?" There were so many people crowded into Carey and Kristie's house, I could not see them all. "Did you hear the debate?"

"I was, and I did."

"What do you think?"

"I thought you were unusually quiet."

"I need to go back and get Alex." I wait to see how John will respond to this. He does not even appear to be surprised. "Did they tell you?"

"Berk told me his thoughts about this. But I want to hear yours."

I tell John everything I know about Athens and about Alex. I tell him my plan to find the entrance. I tell him about my dream.

"And if you find this entrance, how will you find Alex

without being caught? And if he is under the king's influence, how will you convince him to escape?"

I have thought of all this. But I have no answer. "The alternative is to wait here for an attack that will surely kill us all."

John is silent, his eyes closed, as if he's truly considering my idea. Minutes pass. When he opens his eyes, they are clear, bright. He leans toward me. "What if, instead of sneaking in, you walk in?"

"What?"

"I have been praying all night," John says. "I agree that you must go back. Waiting is not beneficial. But no more deception. I think you should walk right up to the gate and request an audience with the prince."

"The guards will kill me before I even speak a word."

"That's possible." John nods. "But they might do the same were they to catch you trying to sneak in. Or trying to speak to the prince. Or trying to sneak him out. Right?"

Of course he is right. "So you think I should just walk over there and knock on the gate?"

"I think you should take a horse and ride up to the gate."

He says it as if it's not a life-threatening proposition. "I cannot ride a horse."

"Sure you can." John smiles. "It's easy."

I think of all the times I questioned John's sanity while we were still in the State. And I think of all he has taught me and my confidence in the fact that he is most certainly sane. And wise.

"What will I tell the others?" I think of Berk. He will never agree to this plan.

"Let me handle the others."

"How will I get a horse?"

"There happens to be one just outside." John winks at me.

After John leaves, I bathe and dress. I think of the last time I went to Athens on my own. It seems a lifetime ago. I pray I have another lifetime to spare.

CHAPTER FORTY-EIGHT

Horses are terrible transports. I like them when I am beside them, feeding them apples. But sitting on top of them . . . why would anyone willingly do this? The entire lower half of my body is sore. As the horse goes faster, I am jostled up and down on this hard saddle. I try to keep my arms relaxed at my sides, the way John showed me, but when it goes too fast, I am forced to pull back on these reins. This is so much different than holding on to the ropes behind the chariot. At least in that, I was standing, not sitting. My legs were not forced to straddle a hairy beast, who could, at any moment, fall or jump and kill me.

But at least I am not walking. Even with last night's sleep to aid me, I would not be able to make that return trip on foot. The days without food in the black chamber have taken their toll on my body. I cannot stop eating. John packed me bread and cheese and a container of milk. I am trying to save some, but I am so hungry. I force myself to put the food away. Fear of eating with only one hand on the reins protects me from completely succumbing to the temptation to eat everything in the sack at my side.

How I was able to ride out of New Hope with no one seeing me or stopping me, I do not know. John simply walked out with me, holding the horse. He gave me some lessons on how to manage the beast, then he sent me off. I looked back once to see him walking back to the village center. No one was around him.

Will Berk be angry when he finds out where I've gone? Maybe he is still upset with me. He shouldn't be. If anyone has the right to be angry, it is me. But I do not want to think about that now. I ride over a hill and see the walls of Athens looming in the distance. I do not know what to do. How far should I go before I stop? My thoughts are interrupted by a shadow hovering over me. The sun is bright today with no clouds on the horizon. I look up to see what caused the shadow. I pull back hard on the reins when I realize what it is: a transport. *My* transport. The one I rode here when I first came to Athens. When Alex rode up to me on his horse. The transport moves backward, but it remains high above my head.

"You were told to leave." Alex's voice drifts down. The transport does not move.

I pull harder on the reins and the horse stops. I swing one leg around and slide down the horse to the ground.

"Why are you here?"

I think of our first meeting. In this very spot. He sounded angry, firm then. Now he sounds tired. And distant.

"I came to speak to you."

"Your words are full of lies." Alex spits out the last word like it is poison. "You killed my sister."

"If you truly believed that, you would have killed me before I ever left Athens."

The transport drops down, and Alex points a weapon at my chest. "It wasn't my choice to spare you."

I see the same hatred in his eyes that I saw at the funeral. Berk is wrong. Alex truly believes I killed his sister. He is not part of the king's plan. He is one of the king's pawns. Just like me.

"Your father lied to you, Alex." I look him in the eye, willing him to listen to me.

"No. I've known him far longer than I've known you. You are the liar. Not him."

His eyes are glazed over, drugged. How much of the medicine has he been given, and how long until he recovers?

"Don't you remember what we talked about?" I take a step closer. He will not discharge the weapon. I am sure of it. "How we planned to help negotiate peace with New Hope? How we were going to go there after our wedding?"

"I remember the lies you fed me." Alex does not move. "I remember seeing you shoot my sister."

"No, Alex." I remain still. "I cared for Helen. She was kind to me. She was good. I wanted to help her."

"You killed her."

"The king had her killed. Just as he planned."

The air around me explodes. Alex discharged the gun. I look down, unsure if I have been hit or not.

"That was a warning." Alex glares at me, weapon still raised. "Say that again, and I will not miss."

My heart is beating so fast, I have trouble speaking. But speak I must. I did not come all this way to be frightened away by this. "Please. Think back to that moment. Do you recall seeing me at the trial?"

"Of course I do."

"I was restrained."

Alex's eyes widen, just for a moment. "Impossible."

"My hands were fastened behind my back." I stare into Alex's eyes. "Just like the other prisoners beside me."

"No." Alex says this with less conviction than before. I have hope that, perhaps, the truth is more powerful than the drugs.

"I was a prisoner." I take another step forward. "Are prisoners allowed access to weapons?"

"You are deceitful." Alex waves me back with his weapon. "You tricked the guard into undoing your restraints. You stole the weapon from him."

"Remember that moment, Alex. You were looking at me. I was restrained." I pray Alex does not choose to kill me for these words. "A guard shot Helen. He stood beside me, fired the weapon, dropped it, and ran off."

Alex stands frozen. He is remembering. I can see it in his eyes. They are darting back and forth. He swallows hard, his Adam's apple bobbing, his eyes closed.

"You remember?"

"No." His voice wavers. "It is not possible."

"You are stronger than the drugs, Alex." I speak softly. "You *can* remember."

Alex slowly lowers the weapon. I do not move.

"How do I know what you say is true?"

I understand how he is feeling. In the State when I was in the Progress simulation, I truly believed I was in a village aboveground. I cared for the people there. I tasted their food, smelled their air. I was sure it was real. And when I discovered it might not be, my world felt shaken. When what feels so real is discovered to be false, reality seems impossible to discern.

"You know what is real." I look into his eyes, as blue as the sky. My heart softens.

"You came here as a spy." His eyes harden again. "I know that."

"That is true." I lower my gaze. "But I did not come to harm you. The people of New Hope want peace. I was sent as a kind of ambassador."

"You told us you came as a refugee from the State."

"I did. I escaped from the State." Even as I say it, I know I am justifying my lies. I cannot do that. "I'm sorry. You're right. I went to New Hope after my escape. And I lied to you because the people of New Hope are afraid of Athens. Much damage has been done to them. Their crops have been stolen, their people injured. They live in fear of this city."

"As they should." Alex stands taller, his eyes darkening.

"No." I stare back into Alex's face. He has to see reality. Truth. "You know that ruling by fear is not ideal. You know your father killed your mother. Planned to kill your sister."

Alex is deathly silent, and I am afraid I have gone too far. I do not move, barely breathe.

"How did you know he killed my mother?"

"Helen told me."

"She must have trusted you."

"She told me about Peter too," I say. "She said you disapproved."

"Of course I disapproved," Alex bites out. "She was a princess."

"Not according to your father."

Alex sighs. "She did not deserve to die."

"I could not agree more. She was kind, beautiful, and caring. She deserved a life of freedom."

Alex's eyes close. "I tried so hard to protect her."

"There is nothing you could have done." I put a hand on his arm. He flexes his muscle, begins to pull away, but then relaxes. "But you can do something for the people of New Hope."

"Why should I do anything for them?"

"Because they have done nothing but try to live out their lives in peace. When have they attacked Athens? What have they done to antagonize you?"

Alex blinks several times. "They withhold their crops."

"Your soldiers take the crops by force." I motion behind me. "They take what is theirs and give nothing in return."

"They came here ready to attack."

"No, they came here to defend Berk and me." I am speaking quietly now, standing just inches from Alex. "They came because they are friends and they were willing to risk their lives to save ours."

Alex is processing this information. How long he has had the drugs in his system, I do not know. How powerful they are, I do not know. I do know that truth sets us free, and I am telling him truth. I am believing that is more powerful than even the Athenian pharmaceuticals. I pray I am right.

"You were our friend." Alex is saying this as if a memory is resurfacing.

"I *am* your friend."

Alex puts a hand on my cheek. He challenges me with his eyes. When I do not look away, he sighs, his thumb caressing my jaw. Suddenly he looks behind him. "They will see you here."

"Who?"

"The guards. They are always watching."

He believes me. He is willing to work with me. I want to jump up and shout, but Alex's face is so serious, our situation is so precarious, and I cannot.

"You have to leave." Alex glances toward the wall, drops his hand, and steps back.

"Come with me. Remember our plan? Your father will not attack if you are in New Hope."

"It won't work. Father made his plan. Nothing will stop him from carrying it out. Nothing."

"But the people of New Hope—" I do not like the look of despair that has settled into Alex's eyes.

"They have days left."

"No." My heart drops. "Alex, we have to do something. They are innocent. Like Helen, like your mother. We cannot allow him to destroy an entire village."

Alex looks back at Athens. I follow his gaze. "You're right. We cannot."

I wait for Alex to speak, but he says nothing. He puts a hand to his head and groans. I don't know what to do, how to help him. I don't know what he is thinking. I place my hand in his. He squeezes so hard I feel like my fingers will break.

"There is only one way to save them." Alex releases my hand. "We must kill the king."

CHAPTER FORTY-NINE

cannot kill anyone. I cannot. Even knowing how evil King Jason is, knowing his plans to destroy the people of New Hope. And Alex cannot kill him. That is his father. Alex loves his father.

I am thinking all of this while lying in a ball beneath Alex's tunic. He has hidden me here, on the transport. I don't know how we will get into the palace without being seen. Alex is planning to take the transport all the way to his room. But he does not fly it very well. This was his first time out with it. His father sent him on a test run to see how high it will go and how fast. Engineers are working to create more of these for the army.

Every time we make a turn, the transport dips and I am sure I will fall off. I hold on to Alex's foot, which is also beneath the tunic. But if I pull too hard, we will fall. And right now, we are above the city walls. I do not wish to fall from this height. So I hold on lightly and pray for a quick, safe landing. And I pray no one who sees us will question why Alex's tunic is lying on the bottom of the transport in a human-shaped lump.

"Excellent." I hear the king's voice from far below. "It climbs higher than I expected."

"Yes, sir." Alex tries to sound happy. "Maneuvers well."

"Better than a horse?"

"Much," Alex calls back.

"Come down here. Let me take a look."

I panic. If the king gets on the transport, we will surely be discovered.

"I wish to try one more thing, Father, before I return it." Alex sounds like a little boy.

"Very well." The king laughs—Alex's act fooled him.

I sigh, then grab hold of Alex's ankle as he lowers the transport for what I assume is the descent into the palace.

I think of my horse. It is returning, hopefully, to New Hope without me. Alex said the guards would have seen it and seen him talking with its rider. But it would be too great a distance for them to discern who it was. He is sure they would not even be able to tell it had no rider on the return trip. I hope he's right. And I hope those in New Hope will not think the worst when the horse returns without me. I do not need them returning to Athens. Their presence would only serve to prevent us from achieving our goal.

I swallow as I think again of what that goal is: killing

the king. I do not want that to be the solution. I want there to be another option. But Alex insists there is not. We cannot imprison the king—the people will revolt. We cannot reason with him. We cannot even speak to him about this. He cannot find out I am here and that Alex is no longer under his control. The transport drops to the ground. Alex steps off, opens a door, and then propels the transport through. I almost roll off as the transport tips to fit through the doorway.

The door closes, and Alex takes the tunic off me. I stand and stretch—my muscles are doubly sore. Alex's room looks the same. It seems wrong that it should be so familiar. So much has changed since I was last here—telling him the truth about my coming to Athens, him telling me what his father planned, discussing our marriage. That seems more like a dream than a reality.

I turn to find Alex's gaze on me. "Thank you."

"For what?" I think of the danger I am placing him in, of all the pain he has endured.

"For coming back." Alex takes a step closer and takes my hand in both of his. "For believing in me."

"You will be a wonderful king." I place my other hand on Alex's arm. "I am proud to know you."

Alex crushes me to his chest before I can take a breath. "Thalli, when this is all over, will you—?"

A loud knock at the door interrupts and causes him to pull away from me. He rushes to the door to make sure it's locked, and then he returns to my side.

"Do not say anything. Do not leave this room until I return," Alex whispers.

I nod, the reality of what we are doing, what I have done,

making my heart pound. Alex motions me to go under the bed. "Hide there until I come back. Servants might come in to clean. It's the safest spot."

There is another knock, louder this time, and I drop to the ground as quietly as I can and crawl far into the shadows.

"Who is it?"

"Your father."

How could he have arrived here so quickly? He was outside the palace just minutes ago. Perhaps there are even more secret passages than I'm aware of.

"Come in." Alex sounds relaxed, though he must be as nervous as I am. I hope the king cannot read in his eyes the truth of what is happening.

I hear the door close and heavy feet shuffle across the floor.

"The guards told me they saw you speaking with someone outside the city."

"Some grunt from New Hope." Alex says the words he rehearsed. "He wanted to discuss peace, beg for mercy. I told him to go away."

"Excellent." The king draws out the word. I see his feet, so close I can touch them.

"And that is all?"

"You want to know the entirety of the conversation?" Alex asks.

"Not necessarily." The king moves away. I cannot see his feet, but I can hear his footsteps. Firm. Frightening. "But the guards said they believed the rider to be inexperienced. And female."

"The guards were far away." Alex does not allow any hint of fear to color his voice. "I was up close."

"You have been deceived by those from New Hope before."

"I will not be deceived again, sir." Alex moves now too.

"Have you used this sword, son?" I hear a metallic scrape. I recall seeing a long sword hanging on the wall above the fireplace in Alex's room.

There is a long pause before Alex speaks. "No."

"*I* have used this sword. I have used many weapons."

"Yes, sir."

"If you are to take my place someday, you must do the same."

"I know, sir."

There is silence. I want to peek out from under the bed, to know what is happening. But I wait, praying Alex is safe.

"You have murder in your eyes." The king's voice is low and deep. My blood freezes with each word.

"As you have taught me, Father."

Something has changed. This conversation is no longer casual. There are threats in the king's tone and defiance in Alex's.

"Do not follow in the footsteps of your mother." Metal slides against metal once again. "Do I make myself clear?"

"Of course." The king is gone for several minutes before Alex speaks again.

"Thalli." He looks under the bed, his gaze meets mine. "We do not have much time."

CHAPTER FIFTY

have been in Alex's room for an entire day. Under his bed. Servants have come and gone, but Alex has not returned since the conversation he had with his father. I imagine all kinds of scenarios. Alex is dead. The army is destroying New Hope. I am powerless, cowering in this room. Doing nothing.

Alex made me swear not to leave. Not under any circumstances. But if he is unable to return for me, am I still bound to that promise? I pull myself out from under the bed and look around. The door is shut tight, no lights are on, and the curtains are drawn. A tiny sliver of light peeks out from between the two dark panels of the curtains. Enough for me to see where

I am going. I stand and stretch. The food Alex left for me sits heavily in my stomach.

I move as quietly as I can to the windows and part the curtains just enough to see out the window. The courtyard is busy but quiet. People—mostly men—move with purpose. They wear a uniform of gold and purple made from a shiny material. One of the Athenian synthetics, I am sure. I do not see Alex or the king. But I did not expect to see them. The king is likely in his chamber. At least I hope he is. I pray he is not moving toward New Hope. I hope the army is still preparing. That Alex is able to stop them long before they leave Athens.

Alex's first goal was to find the contraptions that release drugs into the crowd. The people of Athens must be allowed to think on their own. Alex himself must be protected against the pharmaceuticals. Given another dose, he could reveal our plan, my hiding place, everything.

I pray again that Alex was able to accomplish that goal without being discovered. I try to see into the men's faces below, to see if they appear drugged or clear eyed. But I am too far above them.

I hear the door open, and I scramble to hide behind the curtain. I hold my breath and pull my feet as close to the wall as I can without falling.

"Thalli," Alex whispers.

I release my breath and step out from the curtains. "Were you able to find the boxes?"

"Yes." Alex walks to me and we sit on the couch. "I waited until everyone was sleeping. Father insisted his army rest well for the coming battle. When all was quiet, I snuck into the hall that houses the pharmaceuticals."

"Where is it?"

"Here in the palace. Father wants it nearby so he can access it whenever he deems necessary."

"How did you get in?"

"Father showed me last year." Alex rubs his eyes. "Part of my training. He explained the purpose behind the drugs and how they aid in controlling the people."

"Despicable."

"Yes, but it fits with his ideals." Alex's voice is sad. "He truly believes that is what's best for the people."

I cannot imagine the battle raging in Alex's mind right now. I bite my lip to remain silent. What right have I to offer any advice?

"There is a royal entrance known only to Father and me. It bypasses the guards and leads straight to the storage facility. I removed all the medicines from the boxes and diluted them with water."

"Will that work?"

"I believe so." Alex leans back against the couch. He looks exhausted, deep circles weighing down his eyes. "There was no other option available. The drug activates when airborne. If I discarded it, I would have been infected."

"Now what?"

"Father plans to head to New Hope tomorrow evening." Alex puts his head in his hands. I can barely hear the next words. "I must stop him before he goes."

I place my hand on Alex's back, rubbing his sore muscles. I think he is crying, but even if he is, I am sure he would not want me to acknowledge it. "You should rest."

"I can't sleep."

"Your father is right about this." I stroke his hair. "You cannot fight if you are not well rested."

Alex removes his hands, wipes his face, and looks at me. His blue eyes search mine. He holds my face in his hands. There is such strength and such tenderness in his touch, in his gaze. "Thank you."

I want to know more—what is the army doing? What are they planning? What was the king saying when he was here yesterday? Does he suspect the truth? But I remain silent. Alex is burdened enough. I do not want to add to it.

He drops his hands, stands, and walks to his bed. He does not even remove his shoes. He pulls the bedclothes over him, covering even his face. I hear soft sobs and go sit beside him, pulling the covers down so I can see his face. The pain in his eyes makes my breath catch. I run my fingers through his hair, over and over again.

He closes his eyes, his breath ragged, then calming, calming, until he is asleep. I stroke his face, then tuck the covers around his shoulders. He is so strong yet so vulnerable. I wish I could take away his fears, his hurt. But I cannot. So I pray. I pray for a dreamless sleep. For strength to do what he must do. I return to my spot beside the window, watching the army prepare for a battle I pray they will not fight.

CHAPTER FIFTY-ONE

Several hours have passed. Night has fallen. I pray once again that the king's plans will be thwarted, that the people of New Hope will be saved, and that an alliance, not a rivalry, will be established between these two places I have come to love.

I think of Dallas and little Nicole, their grandparents and parents. That is just one family. There are dozens like them, with relationships and shared memories, love and laughter and dreams of a future. I want desperately to help give them that future. I cannot bear the thought of the alternative.

I hear the sound of a weapon being discharged outside

Alex's door. I swallow back a scream, jumping up from the couch to face the door. Alex jumps out of his bed so quickly, the bedcovers trip him. He catches himself with his hands, peels the covers off, and moves toward the door.

"Wait." I run to Alex, whose hand is on the doorknob. "Do not open it. You don't know who is out there."

Alex is half awake, blinking, his breathing fast. "Someone is shooting."

"And if you run out there, you could be a casualty." I put a hand on his shoulder.

Alex puts his ear to the door. He doesn't need to. The voices out there are loud.

"Stop him." I assume one of the guards shouts out.

"Stay here." Alex pushes me back and then opens the door with the confidence of a prince. "What is happening?"

I do not hear the reply because I am at Alex's wardrobe, rifling through his clothing. I will *not* stay here. But I will disguise myself as best I can. I find a training uniform. If I stuff my hair beneath the helmet, keep my head down, I could pass as a soldier. It worked with Helen. I creep to the door and open it just enough to see out in the hallway. The commotion traveled past here, down the hall—toward the king's chambers.

I follow Alex's example and push the door open and walk out like I belong in the hallway. But no one is there. A crowd of guards gathers at the bottom of the stairs that lead to the king's chambers. There is more shouting. A shot. A shout. Another shot.

Then silence.

"Get out!" Alex's scream is so loud, he sounds as if he is standing right beside me. "All of you. Out!"

At first no one moves. But then the crowd backs up. I am pressed into a doorway—Helen's doorway—as soldier after soldier scrambles back, turns, and walks toward the stairs that lead to the grand hall. Their faces are stunned. Shocked. Something terrible has happened.

I do not say anything. I do not move. No one notices me here, tucked into a doorway. So many soldiers. Why were they all here? Where did they come from? And what happened?

I wait until I am sure no more soldiers will come through. I listen for Alex's voice, for the king. Nothing. Is Alex hurt? That thought propels me forward, up the stairs, to the king's door. At first I see nothing. The window is wide open, along with the curtains. The light is so bright, my eyes cannot adjust. But I smell metal. And fire. And something else. Blood.

My eyes finally adjust and I see Alex. He is kneeling on the floor covered in blood. Below him, eyes wide and staring blankly at the ceiling, is the king.

CHAPTER FIFTY-TWO

What happened?" I look at Alex, but he is focused on his father. He is crying, not even attempting to hide his grief. He does not look away but he does point. I follow his finger to the side of the room, beneath the window.

"Peter." I rush to his side. He has been shot just below his chest. I cover the wound with my hand, but blood seeps between my fingers.

"For Helen," he whispers.

"You killed the king for Helen?" I stroke damp hair away from his face.

"He . . . killed . . . Helen."

"I know."

"No. More. Killing." Every word is an effort.

"Are there others here?" I think of Berk, of Carey and Kristie. Did they bring their own army?

"No." Peter's breathing is labored. "I came alone. Secret entrance."

He found the entrance Helen told me about. "What can I do?"

"Take me to her chamber." Peter tries to sit up, but his face turns deathly white.

"You cannot move, Peter."

"I am dying." With a deep breath, he seems to regain some strength. "Please don't make me die in this room."

Alex is still frozen in grief, in shock. I remove my hand from Peter's wound. His shirt is soaked in blood. He will not make it to Helen's room. It is impossible. But how can I do anything but try to grant him his dying wish?

I bend down behind Peter and try to lift him. I cannot. He places his hands at his sides, and with an effort that costs him precious minutes of life, he assists me. When he is standing, I come to his side, holding him up.

We barely make it down the stairs. I am sure he will collapse with every step. But he keeps walking. I lean my whole side against him as I reach with one hand to open Helen's door. I walk him to her bed, then lay him down on it.

"Smells like Helen." Peter smiles one last time, closes his eyes, and is gone.

: : :

I cannot leave Peter. Not yet. Not like this. I go into Helen's bathing room and wet a cloth. I remove the soiled shirt and clean Peter's chest, face, and hands. It takes several trips, several cloths. The hole the weapon carved into Peter's abdomen stops leaking blood. I think of the sacrifice he made. The love that impelled him to do this. I cannot save him. I cannot even bury him. So I do the only thing I can.

Finally he is clean. I place the covers from Helen's bed over his body. I close my eyes. I wish John were here. He would know what to say to the Designer. I have no words. My heart feels as cold as Peter's skin. As empty as his eyes. I want to stay here, to hide from the pain I know Alex is feeling. But I cannot stay. Alex needs me.

The hallway is still empty, as is the hallway leading to the king's chamber. There is very little noise outside.

The king is dead.

I enter the king's room, and Alex is in the same spot as when I walked with Peter out of the room. This time, though, Alex looks at me.

"I couldn't stop him," he says, his eyes on the still form of his father.

I gaze at the window. Peter must have entered through there. I walk over—there is a balcony that overlooks the city wall. I see a length of fabric looped around one of the columns. Peter threw it up from below, scaled the wall, and broke through the window. I am not glad Peter died. But I am glad someone else killed the king. Alex could not have lived with himself had he done this.

"You need to leave." Alex has no emotion in his voice. He continues to stare blankly, not meeting my eyes. "I will show you the exit. No one needs to know you were here. We will hold the funeral for my father, then I will be made king. After that, I will come to New Hope. There will be peace."

Alex says nothing more. There is no joy in knowing he will rule Athens, no joy in knowing New Hope is saved. His father is dead. His mother, his sister . . . both dead. I do not understand family, but I do understand that losing people you love is incredibly painful.

I follow Alex into the king's wardrobe. There is a panel in the back that leads to a hallway. We walk through that hallway, down stairs, around corners. It is silent and cold. We reach a wall.

"I do not have a horse for you." Alex sounds as if he is miles away. "I am sorry."

"I want to walk." I touch his shoulder. "It will be all right."

I turn to leave, but Alex grabs my hand, turns me around. He is coming out of shock. His eyes change, his face drops as the reality of what happened comes crashing in on him. I pull him to me, and his head falls onto my shoulder.

He grips me tightly, his arms around my waist. He breathes in deeply, then releases a sob. His whole body is shaking, and I fear I cannot hold his weight. He can barely stand. I bend my knees and we sink to the floor, holding each other.

He is weeping, heartbroken. I can only imagine what is in his mind right now. I run my hands through his hair, down his back. I wish I could take away his pain. But I can do nothing. Tears fall down my cheeks, but I hang on to Alex. We sit there until we hear guards shouting his name. Alex pulls away and wipes his face with his palms.

"I should go." I stand, feeling empty and cold as I move away from Alex.

Alex stands as well. He looks toward the hallway and then back at me. With a nod, he pushes a stone on the wall and the evening sky welcomes me—outside the walls of Athens, back to New Hope.

CHAPTER FIFTY-THREE

Why didn't you tell me you were leaving?" Berk does not even greet me.

As soon as I entered the city, crowds gathered around me, asking all kinds of questions. I cannot answer them yet. I asked to be alone. So I returned to my room in Carey and Kristie's house. But Berk followed me.

"I couldn't tell you." I look at Berk. His face is hard, angry. "You would have stopped me or followed me."

"Of course I would have." Berk's eyes soften just a fraction. I can see the battle taking place behind them. "You should never have gone to Athens alone. Again."

"I had to."

"No, you did not." Berk rarely raises his voice, but he is raising it now. "They want nothing more than to kill us, and they will use you to find out how best to do it."

"They will not kill us." I think of all that happened in Athens, all I have yet to tell the people of New Hope. I think of Alex watching me as I left. Heartbroken. Alone. "Please, I need to be alone, just for a while. Then I will tell you everything."

Berk's face falls. "You used to tell me everything without me having to ask."

I want to comfort him, but something holds me back.

"I thought you might want this." Berk reaches into a large bag slung over his shoulder and pulls out a violin. It is older, like the one from the music room in Athens. It is not in good shape, but it looks beautiful to me.

I take the instrument from his hands. His fingers brush mine, and I feel the connection we have always had there, in that touch. I want to tell him everything will be fine, that all will be the way it was. But I cannot say that. I do not know that.

Berk leaves and I shut the door behind him. I wipe down the surface of the violin. I wish I had oil to rub life back into the dried wood, new strings to replace the old. But I hear the music in my mind before I even lift the instrument to my chin, and I thank the Designer for this gift.

I close my eyes and ignore that the violin is slightly out of tune, that the sound is not exactly what I would like it to be. I think back to my violin, perfectly tuned, beautiful, well kept, but trapped in the State. Like I was. I decide the imperfections of this violin, stored in the freedom of New Hope, are far more beautiful.

I play Athens, my imprisonment and false accusations. I play Helen's murder. I play the king's death, Peter's sacrifice. And throughout, I play Alex. He is a melody that repeats in every refrain, in every movement of my bow. I see him bending over the still form of his father, grief and relief battling in his face. He has suffered so much. I play the comfort I would like to give him, the hope for a better future I want him to have.

I finish playing and I feel the peace that always comes with playing music for the Designer. I close my eyes in thanks. I want to play more, to stay longer, to be alone with this violin, alone with the Designer. But I cannot. I must leave this chamber. I must tell the others what happened. They deserve to know they are safe. They deserve to know Peter paid the ultimate price for their safety. I caress the violin once more before placing it on the sleeping platform and moving toward the door.

Never has good news seemed so difficult to deliver.

CHAPTER FIFTY-FOUR

Diana knew Peter was dead. I do not know how, a sense that siblings have perhaps. But when I went to her, she looked at me, heartache in her eyes.

"As soon as he found out what happened to Helen, he knew it was the king's decision," Diana says. "Helen told Peter about her biological father. He knew the king planned to kill Helen."

"I'm so sorry."

"Tell me what happened." Diana wraps her arms around herself. "Everything."

I think of Peter, blood seeping from his body, that last moment as his life drained from him. "He was very brave."

"I know that." Diana closes her eyes. "But I want to know what happened. How did he die?"

I do not want to relive those moments, but I cannot deny Diana the facts she so desperately wants. I tell her everything—how Peter found the secret entrance, how he climbed up the walls of the palace, how he killed the king and was killed by his guards. I tell her how he made his way back to Helen's room so he could die among her things.

"He loved her."

"Very much."

Diana clears her throat. "Too much, I think. If he loved her less, maybe he would still be here."

"Peter did not just avenge Helen." I lean toward Diana. "He saved all of New Hope. He delivered the Athenians from the terrible rule of King Jason. He is a hero."

"I would rather have him here." Diana uses both hands to wipe her eyes and then she stands. "You need to tell the others. They are preparing for battle. They need to know that isn't necessary."

"I will tell them." I stand beside Diana. "They will know what Peter did for them."

"You'll understand if I don't come?"

"Of course."

I leave the room, exit the house. All of the town seems to be waiting outside Diana's door. They are quiet. A few are crying. They have guessed the truth about Peter. They know he left and did not return. They know I insisted on seeing Diana before speaking to them. They know he is dead. I wish that meant I did not have to say the words.

"People of New Hope." I try to speak as loudly as I can, but my voice fails me. "There will be peace."

The people release a collective sigh. There is too much sadness, too much fear for anything more than that. Cheering would be out of place.

I tell them what happened when I returned. I tell them Alex recognized that his father was drugging him, that he knew I did not kill Helen. I tell them he recognized that his father must die. I tell them we were planning just how to commit that assassination when Peter arrived and did it himself.

I wait as the people process this news. "Alex will remain to bury his father and be coronated as king. Then he will come here, to make peace with us."

The people are silent. Some appear afraid to talk; others seem skeptical. A few have tears rolling down their faces. Most, however, look like a massive burden has been lifted from them. They had been planning how to face the wrath of the powerful Athenian army, to be annihilated together, and now they hear there will not be war, but peace.

Kristie steps forward. "We owe Thalli our thanks. She did not mention that she was imprisoned and almost killed, that she was willing to do almost anything in order to procure our peace—including sacrificing her own happiness. She is new to our village, and yet she has given more than most of us ever will. Thank you, Thalli."

A slow clap begins, growing louder. I want them to stop. I do not need applause. I do not deserve it. Peter is dead. Helen is dead. Diana is heartbroken. Had I not come, none of those deaths would have occurred. Perhaps New Hope would have simply gone on the way it had before—bothered by Athens, but not destroyed. I do not feel like a hero.

"May I suggest," John says, stepping forward, "that we gather together to give thanks? I have been working on something. If you would all follow me . . ."

John turns toward an old building in the center of town. It has a tall, sharp cone on its roof and it appears as little used as the music room.

I catch up to John and ask him what this place is.

"A church, Thalli." John smiles up at the old building. "And I will be the pastor."

CHAPTER FIFTY-FIVE

cannot stop thinking about Alex. Even as John shows us the church, as he preaches what he calls sermons to the people, I think about Alex. I listen but I do not hear. Every story reminds me of Alex. I keep picturing him in his room, lying in bed with the covers over his head, crying softly. I do not want him to suffer through this alone. But if I went back, I would create more problems for him. The Athenians surely are angry with New Hope, blaming us for the king's assassination. I would inflame that anger. It's best for Alex that I remain here, to wait for him. But I have to battle within myself to do that.

The church is beautiful. I do not know how John was able to

restore the interior of this building, but every window is clean, the floor shines, and the seats he calls "pews" are oiled and welcoming, if not terribly comfortable. In the front of the church is a raised platform. John stands there and speaks to all who will listen from the Designer's book—a copy he found here. He reads from the psalm he gave me. I pray those words for Alex, that he will find still waters, that his soul would be restored, that he will dwell in the house of the Lord forever.

John concludes and Rhen motions for me to follow her. We walk out of the building toward the orange groves near Dallas and Nicole's home.

"I am worried about John."

"What?" John is happier than I have ever seen him.

"He is not well," Rhen says. "I can tell. He worked too hard on the church. We would have helped. But he told no one."

"I imagine he enjoyed the solitude." I look back at the church. "His communion with the Designer, as he says."

"Perhaps, but he is old, Thalli. Very old. His body cannot do all he wants it to do."

"We'll have to make him slow down, then."

"We can try." Rhen shakes her head. "But the people here have a saying, 'Easier said than done.'"

I laugh. Rhen seems happier too. Her cheeks have color in them and her hair is down.

"Why are you looking at me like that?"

I realize I have stopped and am staring at my friend. "You are beautiful."

Rhen lowers her eyes, her cheeks turning even more pink.

Realization hits me. "I'm not the first person to tell you that, am I?"

Rhen looks ahead, bites her lip. Rhen and Berk will be a good team—like Kristie and Carey. They can be leaders here in New Hope. "It's all right."

"It *is* all right." Rhen says this like it's the first time she has thought it. And it very likely is. My logical friend has always been normal by State standards. Feeling something for Berk is new for her—it would have been unthinkable a few months ago.

"He's a wonderful young man." I am surprised at myself—saying this and meaning it, not choking on the words, not fighting anger or sadness. My time in Athens, with Alex, has changed me in more ways than I realized.

"You hardly know him well enough to make that assessment."

I raise my eyebrows, my calm beginning to dissolve. "I know him better than you may think."

Rhen leans her head to the side—her contemplative posture. "I did not know. Dallas told me you only spoke a few times."

"Dallas?"

Rhen's smile is bright. "Yes. Who did you think I was speaking of?"

I am momentarily stunned. Rhen and Dallas? I think of that young man, his relaxed manner and attitude. When he visited Peter after the house caught fire, Dallas was lighthearted. So different from Rhen's calm and focused personality. Rhen is waiting for me to respond, but the answer to that question comes limping through the groves.

"Thalli." Berk is out of breath, still not completely recovered from his injury. "Can I speak to you?"

Rhen looks from Berk to me, her smile fading. I must be communicating displeasure because Berk's face mirrors Rhen's.

"I will go." Rhen says this as she is walking, her feet barely making any sound as she makes her way quickly through the grove toward the house.

"I apologize." Berk is standing across from me, his hands at his sides, his eyes searching mine. "This has been difficult. More difficult than I imagined."

"You do not need to apologize." I feel almost as if I am talking to a stranger. But Berk is not a stranger. He is the same as he has always been: kind, diligent, controlled. He stayed behind, helped New Hope the same way he helped the State, the same way he helped me. No, Berk is not a stranger.

But I am. I am not the same person I was when we left the State. I am not the same person I was when I left New Hope for Athens. I have changed. But Berk has not. He takes a step closer to me, and I know he does not see that change.

We remain silent. I study the grass at my feet, unsure of what to say. This distance I felt between us is getting wider. I could reach out my hand and touch his hand. I could take one step forward and hold him, lay my head against his chest, and listen to his heartbeat, will the feelings that were always there to resurface. And maybe they will. Maybe I have felt so many emotions over the past weeks that I am spent. There are no emotions left to feel.

"Thalli!" Nicole is running from the direction I just came. She is out of breath, her dark hair damp with perspiration.

I forget Berk for a moment, forget the uncomfortable thoughts invading my mind, and simply smile. I have missed this girl. I reach out to hug her, but the look in her eyes stops me. "It's Mr. John. He's sick. Get Rhen and Dallas. Hurry!"

CHAPTER FIFTY-SIX

I am running as fast as I can. Nicole said that John is by the lake. Baptizing, she said. I don't have time to think about what she means because all I can think of is what she said. John is sick. I think of my podmate Asta. She was sick—the Scientists annihilated her because of it. Rhen was sick too, but she got better. I do not know what other kinds of sicknesses there are. John is old, but he is so happy here in this village, with his church. Those things should bring him health, not sickness.

I am almost at the lake. I see a crowd of people, but I do not see John. Voices are quiet; no one moves. I push myself harder, run faster. I break through the crowd and fall to my knees. John

LUMINARY

is lying on the grass, his face pale, his lips a frightening blue. But he is not frightened.

"I see it." John is whispering, looking into the distance.

"What, John?" I look into the sky, following the path of John's eyes. There are no clouds. The sky is a beautiful blue, and birds are circling above us.

"Heaven."

I am worried. I look at Rhen and Berk, and they are moving toward John. Rhen bends down on the other side of John. She takes his face in her hands. "John, you're not well."

"I am very well." John is still smiling, still looking. "It is time."

My heart constricts. I am not ready to say good-bye to John. I need him. New Hope needs him. "What do we do, Rhen?"

"Don't do anything." John lifts his hand up. I place my hand in his and he squeezes lightly. "He allowed me to see the earth again, to see the sun again. He allowed me to be in a church, to hold his Word in my hands. And he allowed me to see you, following him, growing in him. And now he is allowing me to go home."

I can see the life leaving John. I will it back, but he is so content, so peaceful. It would be cruel to beg him to stay.

"I just wish I could see James." John's voice sounds so far away. "That I could talk to him one more time. I would tell him I forgive him. I love him."

"We need to get him back to the medical center." Rhen motions for Berk and Dallas to help.

"No, please." John waves the boys away. "Let me stay here, by the water, outside. I spent far too much of my life indoors. Let me end my life outdoors."

283

I want to argue, but the facts are glaring. John is dying. But this death is not violent, not bloody like Helen's and Peter's. John is ready, excited. He has longed for this. Rhen and I hold his hands. His face remains toward the sun, his feet touching the water.

"'I have fought the good fight.'" John repeats words he read earlier in church. Words Paul the apostle wrote before his death.

We all gather around John, watching him watch something in the air we cannot see. But he reaches for it, smiles in greeting. He turns to me, his eyes shining. "We will meet again, my dear."

"I know." I wipe a tear from my eye as John turns his face back to the sky.

And then, with a sigh of joy, John is gone.

CHAPTER FIFTY-SEVEN

I play "Jesu, Joy of Man's Desiring" in the front of the church where John stood just the day before. We gathered here for a celebration of John's life. This is what John would have wanted. Not a gathering to grieve, but one of hope. Berk requested I play this.

This is the song that started everything, that led me to the Designer. I heard him in the music. Now I hear him so much more. John told me the words that went with this song, words about drinking from deathless springs. John is doing that right now.

It is hard to grasp that John was just here, and now he is in heaven, with the Designer. I recall that his bride, Amy, walked down the aisle to this song. He cried when he told me that memory, but they were tears of joy. John helped me see the Designer in so much. He helped me to see that music was his language, and that it communicates so much more than words alone. If I had a father, I would have wanted him to be just like John.

When I finish playing, I keep the violin under my chin. I do not want to stop. I do not want this song to end, do not want to acknowledge that this life has ended.

When I finally put the violin down, I see the church filled with people whose lives John touched.

One after another comes to the front with stories of ways John helped them. People I have not met speak of how John came into their homes, talked with them, genuinely cared about their pasts, their dreams, their families. He spoke to each one about the Designer, wanting them to know this God he loved.

The room is silent after several stories, then Gerald walks to the front. This man who had been so angry in that first meeting, wanting to send Diana back, wary of the four of us, is broken, tears streaming into his beard.

"I've never been an easy man." He faces the congregation. I am sitting behind him, watching his head move as he speaks. "But John didn't care about that. He wasn't a bit angry with me for how I talked or what I said about him and his friends. I've never met a soul like him. He walked into my house one day, and I was sure he was gonna start getting onto me, telling me what I should do. But he didn't do that. He walked around my house, looked at my pictures, and asked me about my wife and my kids. We shared stories about life before the War. We talked about music we liked and TV shows we watched. And after about an hour, he looks at me and says, 'Gerald, you don't have a thing to be angry about. You are a blessed man. You should be thanking the Designer every day for what he's given you instead of complaining about what you don't have or what you don't like.' I wanted to get mad at him for that, but he was just too nice to get mad at, ya know?"

The people smile and nod their agreement. I do too.

"We talked for a while longer," Gerald continues. "About all sorts of things. And then he left. But he came back almost every day. I've never known a man like him. He made me want to be a better person."

Murmurs of agreement flow from the crowd.

"I know he is happy to be with his Savior." Gerald nods. "He talked to me about heaven a lot. He sure was excited about that place. I think if he could say anything right now, it would be that we should all be excited for him." Gerald lowers his head and walks off.

I think of John visiting all these people, talking with them and caring for them. The same way he did for me and Rhen and Berk. I think of how I was in Athens trying to help bring peace to New Hope and how John was doing the same here.

The service ends, and we all follow Gerald's horse-drawn truck to the pond where we first saw New Hope. The pond where John dove in to swim and praised the Designer. The men of the city dug a hole just a few feet from the pond. Others have made what they call a casket to house his body, and that is lowered into the hole, then dirt piled on top.

I remain after the others have left. Berk is on my left, Rhen on my right. We do not speak, but neither do we cry. John is finally, truly home.

CHAPTER FIFTY-EIGHT

Alex is here.

He arrived hours after we buried John. Carey and Kristie gathered the people into the church, and we all listen as Alex outlines his plans for peace between the two pockets of survivors. Peace, for the first time in their history.

My mind is full of so many thoughts; my heart is full of so many emotions. I think of John. He is dead. That knowledge brings a feeling far different than what I felt when Helen and Peter died. My heart is not as heavy.

Rhen said that we are not feeling sorry for him—he is where he has long wanted to be. We are feeling sorry for ourselves, for the hole in our lives that he leaves. It is a hole that will never be completely filled. Nor do I want it to be. I do not ever want to forget John, who he was, what he taught me, how he cared for all of us with his gentle, humble way, his faith in the goodness of the Designer. I will carry all he taught me deep within my soul for the rest of my life.

"I do not wish to rule New Hope," Alex says.

I look up at him and another emotion pushes forward, causing my heart to beat faster. The last time I saw him he was battling shock and grief. Today he seems burdened, still, by what seems to be a combined weight of duty and sorrow. He is speaking to everyone, but his gaze locks on mine. "I wish for us to work together. We can unite or remain separate. Whichever you wish. But Athens will no longer make demands of New Hope."

I glance around. The people of New Hope are wary, doubtful. And they have reason to be. Athens has been a violent enemy for most of their lives. This transition will not be easy.

"I have spoken to the leader of our army," Alex continues. "He is aware I am here to make peace. I want to work with your leaders to establish trade rules. I will come here or you may send them to Athens. They are welcome there—you are all welcome there. I hope to learn from your agricultural expertise. You have lived more peaceably than Athens. I want to follow that model. We have been at war far too long."

The people murmur, but no one speaks. I am sure their silence is a result of the somber mood carried over from John's funeral. Could even that timing be from the Designer? We were all here earlier, remembering John, recounting his kindness and love. Those memories hang in the air now. It seems dishonoring to John's memory to even consider arguing or being unkind.

Carey stands beside Alex. "Thank you for coming. Our village, I know, wants nothing more than to live in safety and in peace."

Carey dismisses the people after making plans to reconvene in three days. Alex stays rooted to his spot as many of the villagers come to him, offering him a handshake or a word of thanks. I remain seated, watching, praying, hoping.

When the last villager leaves, Berk touches my arm. I barely noticed him beside me. His gaze darts to Alex, who is also looking at me, then back again. "Thalli, when you were in Athens, with Alex—"

I shake my head. "Nothing happened."

Berk looks at Alex again. "You're not the same as you were when you left."

"Of course I'm not the same." I fold my arms across my chest. "I watched innocent people die because of me. I saw a whole city drugged. I almost died. You almost died. I will never be the same."

"That's not what I mean."

I know what he means, what he is asking. But I cannot discuss it with him. Not now. We both turn as Alex walks toward us.

"Thalli, may I speak with you?" He looks at Berk. "Alone."

Berk stiffens beside me. "She needs to rest. It has been a long day."

"I am fine." I raise my eyebrows at Berk and then turn to Alex. "Of course I will speak with you."

I do not give Berk the opportunity to argue with me. I walk

toward the small pond, Alex following behind me. Neither of us speak. I know Alex is drained—of energy, of emotion. I want to ask him how the people of Athens are, whether or not he told them yet about the drugs, about the murders. How much truth has he revealed? How much does he feel needs to remain concealed? But I do not ask him any of that. I will let him speak when he is ready.

We walk around the pond so that when we sit, we are facing New Hope. I can see the homes, the buildings, the church. People moving around. I can see the fields that surround the village, the animals. I am filled with a sense of belonging like I have never had before. Not in the State, not in Athens. This— New Hope—is home.

"Thalli." Alex's voice is quiet, tired. "I cannot do this."

I look at him. His hair is longer than it was when I first met him. The dark blond curls hang loosely, past his shoulders. There are dark circles under his blue eyes, his mouth sags, as if he hasn't the strength to lift it into a smile. He is wearing black—black tunic, black pants, black boots—all of which adds to the heaviness that seems to surround him.

"Of course you can." I push back a curl that has fallen in front of his face. "But you can't do it all at once. Are you sleeping? Are you eating? You cannot solve all the problems right away."

Alex lifts his face, and agony weights his eyes. "The people are looking to me, and I don't know what to tell them. They don't see me as a person. To them, I am just the king. They will do what I say because they do not know any better. But they will not see me as an equal. They don't treat me as an equal. They fear me, Thalli. Me. And I don't know how to convince them I am not to be feared. I want to be one of them. I want to be part of them. I don't want to be alone in the palace."

"They will see that." I put my hand on his chest. "Give them time."

Alex places his hand over mine and leans in so close, I can feel his breath on my face. "Don't leave me too, Thalli. Please. I need you."

"I will help you however I can."

"Then come back with me." Alex lifts my hand to his mouth, caressing my palm with his lips. "I said once that I didn't know if I loved you. I was wrong. I was ashamed to admit it. Love killed my mother. I did not want to fall prey to that same weakness. But I cannot help myself. I love you, Thalli. So much. I want you to rule with me. By my side. Please say you'll come back with me."

I do not know what to say. He is alone. And he needs me. I look into his blue eyes, and I cannot deny that I care for him. But do I love him? I was ready to marry Alex before to save New Hope. Am I willing to marry him now?

What about Berk? My heart has never felt so torn. My first thought is to ask John what I should do, and my own tears fall as I realize I cannot do that. Ever again. I must decide for myself. I must ask the Designer what he wants me to do.

But I do not have time to say this to Alex because the sky above New Hope suddenly darkens. I look up and see a transport larger than I have ever seen before. I know where it is from and who is aboard.

The Scientists have found New Hope.

CHAPTER FIFTY-NINE

I run back to town as quickly as I can. My side aches but I don't stop. I can't stop. The transport is landing right in front of John's church. Our church.

Townspeople are running outside. I hear some of them shouting that it's an Athenian attack. They look at Alex and me, now standing among them, with distrust, anger.

Dust is flying all around the transport. A long white cylinder seems to be floating just above the ground as it hovers in place, then lands with barely a sound. The people who were shouting just minutes before are now silent, staring at the cylinder.

The front of the transport slides down, creating a ramp to the ground. Dr. Loudin steps out first. He is dressed in Scientist white. An unnatural smile fills his face. He looks at the people, at the church, at the sky.

"Greetings." His accent surprises me. I have grown so accustomed to the manner of speaking here that he now sounds foreign. "My name is Dr. Loudin."

Berk is beside me. Rhen is here too. I did not see them walk up. My eyes were trained on the transport, on the Scientists. I know they are thinking what I am—the Scientists have come to take us, to annihilate us. I look at Berk—the muscles in his jaw are twitching. Rhen appears calm, but I know her mind is working, analyzing Dr. Loudin's appearance, considering what options we have.

"Loudin." Carey walks up to the Scientist. He is not smiling. "What is the meaning of this?"

"Ah, Dr. Jordan." Dr. Loudin is looking at Carey as if through a microscope. I have seen that look on his face before, when he was examining me. When I was his project. "Nice to see you again."

Kristie steps forward and Dr. Loudin's eyes soften, just for a moment. "Kristie."

Kristie meets Loudin's gaze and clears her throat. "Joseph."

"I mean no harm to any of you." Dr. Loudin spreads his arms. "I applaud your obvious ingenuity. You have created beauty from ashes. I would like to do the same."

I look around. The people are staring at the transport, their eyes wide. They are fearful, but they are also in awe.

"May I speak to you?" Dr. Loudin looks from Kristie to Carey. "Privately?"

Carey is reluctant, but Kristie motions Dr. Loudin into her house. As soon as the door is shut, Alex touches my arm. "What does he want?"

I assumed Dr. Loudin came for us, to return us to the State and annihilate us. But he barely glanced at Berk, Rhen, and me. His eyes hardly left Kristie. He knew she would be here. And he wanted to speak to her—and Carey—alone. "I don't know what he wants. But I am sure it is not good."

Berk is on the other side of me, silent. Rhen is quiet as well. The transport looms beside us, a terrifying reminder that our escape failed. I feel the same way I felt in the annihilation chamber and again in the dark cell in Athens: trapped. The longer the three Scientists remain inside, the more my fears increase.

The people around us are talking but quietly. They are afraid, but they are also impressed. They walk around the transport. It is larger than anything Athens has, far more advanced than anything in New Hope. I cannot speak. My throat is tight, my stomach aches. Something bad is happening. I know it. But I cannot stop it.

The door opens—over thirty minutes after the three went in. Kristie's eyes are red. Carey's face is hard, angry.

"People of New Hope." Dr. Loudin addresses the people as if he were an Announcer on a wall screen discussing the news of the day. "I am happy to report that your village and our State will be working together. We will help each other to be better than we are alone. Kristie has agreed to come with me, just for a time, to the State. She recommended Alex join us, as a representative of Athens."

I gasp, grabbing Alex's arm. I do not know what Loudin has

planned, but it is not good. And if Kristie and Alex go, they will not return.

"And Thalli, of course." Dr. Loudin's gaze burns into me. "I have heard of her bravery. She will join us as well. We will make a wonderful team, won't we, Carey?"

Carey doesn't speak. His lips are shut tight. He gives a slight nod, eyes hard. He turns to me and says something with his gaze that I cannot quite grasp. I know, however, I must go. That much is clear.

Dr. Loudin smiles and steps aside. I follow Kristie into the transport. Alex is beside me. I turn to say good-bye to Berk, to Rhen, to my friends in New Hope, but the ramp is lifting, shutting me off from this village.

Berk is yelling for me to stop, demanding to be allowed on board. But the ramp silences his pleas.

We are encased in the transport. Artificial light replaces the sunlight. A door in the side of the cylinder opens and Dr. Williams exits, a needle in her hand. The transport lifts off the ground. Assistants follow Dr. Williams.

I want to run, but there is nowhere to go. I feel my hands pulled behind me. I see Dr. Williams raising the needle, aiming for my neck. I twist and turn. I hear Alex calling my name, but he cannot stop her. I cannot stop her. I see a drop of liquid escape the needle . . . I feel it dig into my skin.

Then my world goes black.

DISCUSSION QUESTIONS

1. Thalli begins this journey upset at being rescued. Why do you think she feels this way? Do you think she is justified in those feelings?
2. What do you think Rhen and Berk were talking about while they were on the transport? Do you think Thalli ever had any reason to be jealous?
3. Imagine you are John—what would it be like to see grass, trees, dogs, and ponds for the first time in forty years? If you were John, what would you have missed the most?
4. Thalli is shocked to discover The Ten were actually Fifteen. What other secrets do you think have been kept from the citizens of the State?
5. In what ways is New Hope different from the State? Which difference do you suppose is the most difficult for the State-born to adjust to?
6. Do you agree with Thalli's decision to go to Athens? Why or why not?

7. John challenges Thalli to trust in the Designer, even in the valley. Have you ever walked through "the valley of the shadow of death"? How did you handle that difficult time? What did you learn from it?

8. What do you think Alex's childhood was like?

9. Discuss the deaths in this story—which were the most difficult to read? How was each one different than the others?

10. Thalli does not get to answer the question Alex posed at the end of *Luminary*. What do you think her response will be?

ACKNOWLEDGMENTS

I am incredibly grateful for the team at Thomas Nelson Fiction. They believed I could write this book even before I did. I am humbled by your faith in me.

My amazing agent, Jenni Burke, helped me create and tweak the proposal that outlined this trilogy. Throughout the process, my editor, Becky Monds, has been part sounding board, part cheerleader, and all friend—thanks for challenging me not to be so easy on my characters! Julee Schwartzburg, as always, saw through my messes into the possibilities and helped me see those possibilities as well. Kristen Vasgaard created the fabulous cover. Laura Dickerson and the whole marketing and sales team worked so hard to make sure this story got into the hands of readers all over the world. Thank you, thank you, thank you!

A special thanks to my friends and proofreaders/previewers: Lauren Webb, Rebekah Kelly, Tammy Norwood, and Kristie

Wheetley. Thanks also to my amazing Sunday school class for praying me through the writing of this novel.

My family, as always, is my greatest inspiration and my biggest fans. My husband, Dave, is one of the best men ever to walk the face of the earth. Our kids, Emma, Ellie, and Thomas, are the most wonderful gifts God has given me.

A huge thanks to you, my readers. Thank you for your e-mails of encouragement, for "liking" me and "following" me. I am so grateful for you.

The reason that I write, that I live and breathe, is because of my wonderful Savior, Jesus Christ. He has made each one of us beautiful anomalies. I pray that every person reading this knows how very special you are to the Designer, how unique and precious and valuable you are to him.

All her life Thalli thought she was an
anomaly. Now she must use her gifts to
fulfill the role she was called to play: Revolutionary.

OVERPOWER.
OVERTHROW.
OVERCOME.

REVOLUTIONARY

KRISTA MCGEE

The conclusion of the Anomaly Trilogy by Krista McGee

Available in Print and E-book July 2014

Dear Readers,

We hope you've enjoyed reading the second installment of the Anomaly trilogy. One of the joys of our role in publishing is connecting talented authors with one another.

Krista McGee and Shannon Dittemore are two leading authors in the young adult space, and it has been so exciting to watch them support each other's work. Krista and Shannon are not only colleagues but friends, and both share a passion for working with young adults. They each believe in the power of story and its ability to inspire and touch readers and wanted to offer a free gift to you within the pages of their books.

We hope you enjoy reading the following excerpt from *Angel Eyes*, the first in the Angel Eyes trilogy by Shannon Dittemore.

Happy Reading!

Your Friends at HarperCollins
Christian Publishing

AN EXCERPT FROM *ANGEL EYES*

BY SHANNON DITTEMORE

Dothan, Israel—2,500 years ago

The boy trembles. Fear wraps him tight, rattling his callow frame.

He sees an army arrived in the dead of night. He sees soldiers flooding the canyon floor, flanking them on every side. Cursing, spitting soldiers, here for his master. The boy sees horses fogging the morning air and chariots pulling men with bows. He sees spears with bronze tips and swords of iron glinting in the predawn light.

And he imagines.

He imagines his master hauled away in chains. He imagines his own blood glazing one of those swords. He imagines death.

Fear does that to the imagination.

"Master," he asks, "what shall we do?"

The prophet wrestles silently with a truth. He knows things the boy does not. Sees things the boy can't see.

He sees the enemy. Oh yes, he sees them. But he sees their forces surrounded. He sees an angelic army. Great winged men with swords of light and halos of gold. He sees them lining the mountains that hem together this canyon. He sees horses emerging from fiery skies and chariots with wheels of sunset cloud. He sees riders with bows drawn and arrows of flame fixed on their adversaries.

And he knows. He knows they're here to protect him. To protect the boy.

Truth does that to the heart.

And the prophet knows this: There's no room here for fear. Only truth.

The boy needs to know it. He needs to know there are things unseen, forces for good and for evil. He needs to know there are more fighting for them than for their enemies.

Day breaks over the horizon, and the prophet lifts up his voice. With a cry to rival the snorting horses and the irreverent soldiers, he prays for his servant.

"Lord, give him eyes that he might see."

And God answers the prophet. By the hand of an angel and a halo of gold, he answers him.

And for the first time in his young life, the boy sees.

1

Brielle

The knot in my throat is constant. An aching thing. Shallow breaths whisper around it, sting my chapped lips, and leave white smoke monsters in the air.

It takes them nine seconds to disappear. Nine seconds for the phantoms I've created to dissolve into nothingness.

How long till the one haunting my dreams does the same?

The absence of an answer makes my hands shake, so I slide the lambskin gloves out of my book bag and put them on.

If only it were that easy.

Like glacial masses shoving along, ice travels my veins, chilling my skin and numbing my insides. Three weeks of this biting cold outstrips the severity of my nightmares, but I haven't suffered enough and I know it.

"Miss, isn't this your stop?" The man's voice skates atop the frozen air.

I want to answer him, but the words don't come. A single tear thaws, escapes the confines of my lashes, and races triumphantly down my cheek. It soaks into my knit scarf—an invisible trail marking its life.

"Miss?" he tries again. "We're here. We've reached Stratus."

My legs are stiff, refusing to stand. I just need a minute. I should say something at least—answer him—but the knot in my throat refuses to budge. I raise a gloved hand to wrestle it away.

"I'm sorry, dear, but the conductor is impatient today. If you don't exit the train, you'll have to ride back to Portland with us."

I turn toward the aisle and look at the poor man. He's sixty at least, with a tuft of gray hair and an oversized bow tie. The kind you only see in the movies. He, too, is wearing gloves, and it's a small comfort to know I'm not the only one chilled. His face wrinkles into a million lines, and the corners of his mouth lift.

"Of course, if you'd like to return with the train, you're more than welcome. I could use the company." He gestures to row after row of empty seats.

"No," I murmur, standing quickly. I cannot return with this train. Not now. Not to the place where it happened. "You're right. This is my stop." I gather my bags and sink deep into my parka before stepping onto the platform.

Why is everything so cold?

I wrap my scarf around my neck once more and think of Hank, a coworker of my dad's, who climbs Mount Hood every year. He's lost all the toes on his right foot to frostbite, and one year a companion fell on the south side of the peak and slid into a crevasse, sacrificed to the god of adrenaline. After losing so much, how can such a journey be worth it?

The train pulls away from the station. It's empty now, but I stare after the steel snake as the heaviness of *good-bye* squirms inside my chest, locked away in a cage of frozen bones and tissue. Will I ever thaw enough to say the word?

The parking lot is small, but as I cross it I cast a flickering gaze at the man standing by a pickup. Six foot five and burly, my father waits with a stubborn smile as I trudge toward him. *Don't come*, I'd said. *I can take a taxi.* I knew he'd be here anyway.

The heavy load falls from my hands. It crunches into the frozen blacktop, and I lean against his truck, counting silently to fifty-eight before he says a word.

"I know you didn't want me to come, Brielle, but you're not in the city anymore. There's just the one cabbie. Didn't want you standing here all night waiting for the guy." He stretches his long lumberjack arms around my shoulders awkwardly. "Plus, I couldn't wait to see you. It's been too long."

He adds the last sentence very quietly, and I pretend not to hear it. The knot in my throat is a traitor, though, and explodes in a gush of air. The sobs that have bruised me from the inside out finally break free as my daddy wraps me in his arms and tucks me into his flannel coat.

He lets me cry, his grip so tight I have to struggle out of it when I'm done. Still snuffling, I wipe my face on my sleeve and crawl into the truck. The scent of wood chips and spearmint gum tickles my nostrils, and I settle back, breathing it deep. Dad drops into his seat, and I have to brace my hand against the door to keep from sliding into him on the sloping bench seat.

"Sorry," he says.

The engine revs, and we leave the parking lot behind us. From the train station it's just three miles to the house I grew up in. The distance flies by, leaving me feeling like an outsider.

I can't point out a single change, but it all feels foreign. The mixture of evergreen trees and cow pastures are a bizarre juxtaposition after the city's skyscrapers and manicured parks.

I don't want to be back here, but the oak tree in our lawn comes into sight and the pain ebbs a bit. The house isn't anything to get worked up over, though I've always been happy to call it home. Ranch-style, white with yellow trim, it sits nestled in a jumble of evergreens. Within, everything about the furnishings is supersized to fit my mountain of a father.

We pull into the long gravel driveway, and I cringe at the ridiculous mailbox that's been added in my absence.

"Where did you get that?"

"I made it," he says, proud of his handiwork. The mailbox is ghastly: a ten-gallon bucket, our last name scrawled across it, perched atop the old post. "Whatcha think?"

"What happened to the old *normal* mailbox?"

"I backed into it with the trailer." He chuckles, and the elastic bands around my heart ease up just a millimeter.

"Well, at least I know what to get you for Christmas."

Dad parks the truck, and a small sigh escapes my lips. I hadn't planned on living here again, ever, and the sting of disappointment jabs at my gut: I did not finish what I set out to do. But I can't go back. I can't. I need this house, and I need my dad.

"Who's living in the old Miller place?" I ask, nodding at the only other house in sight—a farmhouse situated about a hundred yards to the east.

He cranes his neck to look past me. "Don't know. Somebody just moved in."

Several of the windows are alive with light. The truck rattles with the sound of a stereo, and my heart slows to the rhythm of the bass line. Like a metronome, it's soothing, and I lean back against the headrest.

"Ah, heck. I'll go over there after dinner and tell 'em to turn it down."

"No. Don't. Please."

His shoulders sag, and I realize he'll do anything to make me comfortable tonight. We sit in the cab, the rattling truck and bass guitar filling the silence.

"You know, kiddo, you don't have to talk about it. You don't. You don't really need to *do* anything for a while." He's rehearsed this little speech, I can tell. "Just *be*, okay? Be here, and maybe one day you'll see it really wasn't your fault."

I choke a bit and look into his big teddy bear face. He can't know. He's my dad. He sees only what he wants to see. He'll never understand that I could have stopped it. I look out the passenger-side window, over the dead grass and the brown leaves scattered on the ground. I look out at the coming winter and the setting sun and say all I plan on saying about it.

"Ali was eighteen, Dad. My age. A little bit younger, really." My body—my skin, even—feels so heavy with the icy weight of it all. "I could have stopped the whole thing. There's no way around that, but you said it yourself. I don't have to talk about it."

I turn to face my father. He needs to know how serious I am. This subject is off-limits. Until the trial—until I'm sitting on that witness stand—there isn't another soul who needs to hear my story. I look Dad straight in the eye. Tears gather there, they run down his face and sparkle in his beard.

"Okay. We just won't talk about it," he concedes. He kisses my nose. "Some guy named Pizza Hut made us dinner, so let's get to it."

He climbs out and throws a hostile look at the old Miller place. Then he grabs my bags from the bed of the truck and stomps inside.

"Pizza Hut, huh?"

I follow him into the house. His boots leave muddy prints up the porch stairs and across the linoleum floor. I used to reprimand him for stuff like that, but not today. Today, I simply ghost by.

Weaving around the mud splotches, I make my way through the kitchen and into my old room. It's been vacant for two years, and still it looks the same. I pick at a loose thread on my jeans, uneasy at the lack of change. This ancient town is tightfisted with her diversions, and it's quite possible I've had my share. The idea hurts. Like that dingy penny in the bottom of your pocket—the one that must be eighty years old. You scratch away the gummy muck and are horrified to find how new the coin is. Much newer than you ever would have guessed.

How did I get so filthy, so damaged in just a few short years?

I'd been given the chance of a lifetime, and now, two years later, my own inaction had ruined not only my dreams but the life of someone I'd loved. Broken dreams I can handle, but I'd give anything to go back and make things right for her.

That isn't possible, of course. Some things you have to do right the first time. If the past three weeks have taught me anything, it's that.

You don't always get a second chance.

The story continues in *Angel Eyes* by Shannon Dittemore . . .

ABOUT THE AUTHOR

Author photo by Ruth Kegel

When Krista McGee isn't living in fictional worlds of her own creation, she lives in Tampa and spends her days as a wife, mom, teacher, and coffee snob. She is also the author of *Anomaly, First Date, Starring Me,* and *Right Where I Belong.*